Privatizing Russia

Privatizing Russia

Maxim Boycko
Andrei Shleifer
Robert Vishny

The MIT Press
Cambridge, Massachusetts
London, England

HD4215.15
.B69
1995

This book was set in Sabon by Wellington Graphics and was
printed and bound in the United States of America.

Library of Congress Cataloging-in-Publication Data

Boycko, Maxim.
  Privatizing Russia / Maxim Boycko, Andrei Shleifer, Robert
  Vishny.
    p. cm.
  Includes bibliographical references and index.
  ISBN 0-262-02389-X (alk. paper)
    1. Privatization—Russia (Federation) 2. Russia (Federation)—
Economic policy—1991– 3. Capitalism—Russia (Federation)
I. Shleifer, Andrei. II. Vishny, Robert. III. Title.
HD4215. 15.B69 1995
338.947—dc20   94-25308
                                                      CIP

Contents

Preface

In late 1991, a handful of reformers led by Anatoly Chubais embarked on a far-reaching program to privatize Russian firms. At the time, the idea of privatizing Russia seemed to most people to be a pipe-dream. Yet three years later the task was largely done. A large class of owners has been created in Russia. Stock trading has grown rapidly. The restructuring of Russian industry, and the rest of the economy, has begun.

None of this would have happened, we believe, if fundamental economic principles were not deemed as workable in Russia as elsewhere in the world. And none of this would have happened if the Russian reformers had not adapted theoretical principles to political reality.

This book looks at the Russian privatization from our perspective as members of the team that put it together. We show how property rights analysis can be used to explain Russia's socialist experience, the difficulties it faced during the transition to markets, as well as the importance of privatization. We explain why most politicians in transition economies play such a destructive role, and argue that depoliticization of economic life is the principal benefit of privatization. Finally, we describe what actually happened.

Russian privatization could not have had a better champion than Anatoly Chubais, who as both a thoughtful reformer and a skillful politician spearheaded the design, passage, and implementation of the program. His 29-year-old deputy, Dmitry Vasiliev, organized the work on the program and protected its radical ideas from never-ending attacks. Our own involvement started when Chubais and Vasiliev came into office in November 1991. Shleifer met Chubais that November through his colleague Jeffrey Sachs, who at the time was beginning to advise the Russian government on macroeconomic reform. Shleifer then asked Boycko, whom he met at IMEMO, an economic research institute, to work together. The initial group working on the program also included Jonathan Hay, a newly-minted Harvard Law School graduate who wrote many regulations governing the Russian privatization, Albert Sokin, a lawyer with a keen instinct for Russia's treacherous politics, and Pyotr Mostovoy, the adviser to Pyotr Fillipov, privatization's champion in the Russian Parliament. Vishny joined the group a few months later and worked on designing the voucher program.

In addition to developing the privatization program, the core team stayed through its implementation, as well as the follow-up reforms. Vasiliev and Mostovoy, who also became Chubais's deputy, headed the implementation of voucher privatization. Boycko and Hay managed the dozens of Western consultants who came to provide technical assistance with implementation. Boycko became Chubais's principal advisor, as well as the CEO of the Russian Privatization Center, a nonprofit institution established to promote post-privatization restructuring of Russian companies using foreign assistance funds. Vishny continued working with Vasiliev, Hay, and Sokin, who turned their energies to the development of the capital market. Shleifer continued to advise Chubais, and also headed the Harvard Institute for International Development project that delivered strategic support to the implementation of privatization with the financing provided by the U.S. Agency for International Development.

Although this book is in part a history of the Russian privatization, it is also a synthesis of our ideas about it. We have published these ideas in several professional articles, and try to bring them together here. Over the last three years, our research in this area has been supported by the Bradley Foundation, the Russell Sage Foundation, and the National Science Foundation. The writing of this book was supported by the Harvard Institute for International Development.

The Russian privatization effort benefitted from considerable financial support from the United States Agency for International Development, the European Bank for Reconstruction and Development, the World Bank, and the International Finance Corporation. We were fortunate that the representatives we worked with—Gregory Huger and Walter Coles from U.S.A.I.D., Ira Lieberman from the World Bank, Peter Stredder from the EBRD, and Roger Gale from the IFC—were extremely dedicated to the cause of the Russian privatization.

Various parts of this manuscript were read by our colleagues, including Mark D'Anastasio, Robert Bates, Joseph Blasi, Francesco Giavazzi, Oliver Hart, Jonathan Hay, James Hines, Raghu Rajan, and Ilya Segal. We are grateful for their comments. We have also benefitted a great deal from Karen Pennar's editing of the manuscript. Lastly, we would like to thank our families and friends, who had to put up with our frequent travels and long hours over the last three years.

November 1994
Moscow, Cambridge, Chicago

1

Introduction

In November of 1991, fresh from his victories over both the organizers of the Communist coup and Mikhail Gorbachev, President Boris Yeltsin formed his first cabinet. To head it, Yeltsin named Yegor Gaidar, a thirty-five-year-old economist who had achieved some prominence participating in earlier Gorbachev reform efforts, but was by no means a professional politician. Gaidar expected his job to be that of a technician implementing economic reforms. Gaidar in turn named Anatoly Chubais, his friend and a relatively unknown Deputy Mayor of St. Petersburg, to run the State Committee on the Management of State Property (known by the Russian acronym GKI), a small government agency formed earlier that year. In the turbulence of Russian politics, Gaidar and Chubais expected to last only four to five months, even as technicians. They hardly expected that, before long, they would be leading the political charge to bring about the most radical and profound reform attempted in the twentieth century.

The new government knew that urgent action was necessary. Gorbachev left the Russian economy in a sorry state. Five years of ad hoc and timid reforms of industry had introduced severe economic distortions into an already limping economy. For months in 1990 and 1991, store shelves stayed bare as prices remained frozen and the government kept printing money to finance its spending. As the winter of 1991 approached, many people feared famine. To avoid disaster, Western governments shipped food to Russia. Gaidar faced a daunting task: he not only had to eliminate shortages by decontrolling prices, but he also had to deal with budget deficits and the runaway inflation that were certain to follow price decontrol. Price liberalization and subsequent stabilization were his highest priorities. Privatization, in contrast, was not nearly as urgent. After all, even Poland, which managed to subdue inflation, had no luck with privatization. The very name of Chubais's agency reflected ambivalence about privatization both in the government and in the country at large.

Gaidar freed prices on most goods other than energy on January 2, 1992. As expected, shortages disappeared within a few weeks. Yet stabilization eluded Gaidar. Prices rose ten-fold in January of 1992, and continued rising for most of 1992 and 1993 by over 20 percent a month. Even as the macroeconomic situation was deteriorating, however, a quiet effort to transform ownership was gathering force. In the spring of 1992, marshalling support from Gaidar and Yeltsin, Chubais ushered through the government and Parliament a far-reaching mass privatization program that used vouchers to allocate shares in Russian industrial firms to their employees, managers, and the public. The program officially kicked off in October of 1992, and interest in it built quickly and inexorably. By the time it officially ended on July 1, 1994, two-thirds of Russian industry was privately owned, the stock market was booming, 40 million Russian citizens owned shares in privatized firms and mutual funds, and Chubais had become one of Russia's best-known politicians.

Looking back to the fall of 1991, it is hard not to be surprised by what happened. Neither the government nor public opinion saw the need for quick and comprehensive privatization, especially before the macroeconomy was put in order. The predominant Western advice, including that of the World Bank and the IMF, was to achieve macroeconomic stabilization first and to consider privatization later. Many members of the Yeltsin government opposed privatization, and parliamentary support seemed unlikely, especially given the dominant role of the old-guard politicians in the Russian Parliament. Even if legislation on privatization could be forced through, few people could imagine the Russian bureaucracy actually administering a major reform, or the Russian people involving themselves in yet another "government program." Defying this widespread skepticism, Chubais won over the cabinet and the Parliament, created public support for privatization, got the bureaucracy on board, and actually implemented the program.

This book presents the story of Russian privatization from our perspective as key participants. We focus on the ideas that shaped the program, and provide a first-hand account of the economic and political problems that Russia's privatizers tried to address. We also describe how the program worked. We spend relatively little time on the government and parliamentary battles that surrounded the adoption of the program, since those were fought and won by Chubais. The winning of these political battles is probably the most surprising and exciting story of Russian privatization, yet it must await Chubais's memoirs. This book, then, deals with the ideas behind Russian privatization, and shows how these ideas worked in practice. We write it in part as a history of a remarkable reform, and in part to show that basic economic principles work well, even, and perhaps especially, in Russia.

1 Russian Politics

To comprehend the sheer improbability of Russian privatization and to put the rest of the book in context, it is necessary to briefly review Russia's politics between the fall of 1991 and the fall of 1994. In November of 1991, Yeltsin came into power riding a tide of great expectations for both economic and political change. He was supported by the majority of the people. The three-year-old Russian Parliament, led by a new speaker, Ruslan Khasbulatov, professed loyalty to the President and granted him "extraordinary powers" to conduct reforms. Unlike the reformers in Eastern Europe, Yeltsin neither staged a political purge, nor called for new parliamentary elections. Instead, along with reformers, Yeltsin kept a variety of old-guard ministers in his cabinet. His approach was one of reconciliation.

With Yeltsin's support, Gaidar immediately started reforms. He freed almost all prices, liberalized trade, sharply cut defense expenditures, and denied easy credits to large state firms. The political conflicts started immediately. The old directors of state firms, none of whom lost their jobs when the government changed, immediately ignited a parliamentary attack on reforms. Khasbulatov made his first demand for the resignation of the government in January of 1992. As political tensions mounted, the G-7 group of industrial countries in April announced a multi-billion-dollar aid package for Russia, including badly needed food assistance, trade credits, and stabilization funds. In late May, Yeltsin also fired some reformers (though not Gaidar), and appointed several new deputy prime ministers with a deeper appreciation for the problems of industry, including the future Prime Minister Viktor Chernomyrdin. These changes temporarily appeased the Parliament, although Russian reformers got a new enemy, Yeltsin's Vice President Alexander Rutskoi, an Afghan-war hero who called Gaidar and his fellow reformers "boys in pink pants."

Much of the privatization legislation went through the government and the Parliament in the spring and summer of 1992. When given an opportunity, the Parliament modified the privatization program for the worse, but did not kill it. Why is it that this group of ex-communist politicians and industrial lobbyists allowed privatization to proceed? Perhaps the best explanation lies in Chubais' political skills, a combination of coalition-building, recognition of the special interests of managers and workers, compromise, and appeal to the public. That and Yeltsin's support at critical junctures won both public and interest-group support of privatization and thus ensured the program's passage.

But it probably also helped that the Parliament did not take privatization seriously in the spring of 1992, since it looked too implausible in a country like Russia, with old state directors maintaining close political ties to the government and obtaining ever-increasing subsidies. After the privatization program passed the Parliament, the hard-liners realized that Chubais was for real, and began a much more active campaign against both him and privatization. As a result, every subsequent major regulation of privatization was introduced by Presidential decree rather than parliamentary action.

In late summer and fall of 1992, the conflict between Yeltsin and the Parliament heated up yet again. In July 1992, the Parliament appointed a new central bank governor, Viktor Gerashchenko, who immediately began to issue vast amounts of chcap credits to firms. Gaidar by that time was no longer able to control spending, and inflation spun out of control. In the meantime, Yeltsin introduced the final elements of the privatization program by decree, and announced the introduction of vouchers in August, in a major speech commemorating the defeat of the communist coup a year earlier. In October, the distribution of vouchers to the population started and privatization got seriously underway. Finally, in December of 1992, as Yeltsin's "extraordinary powers" expired, the Parliament won a major victory by forcing Yeltsin to fire Gaidar and replace him with Chernomyrdin, the former minister of oil and gas. When historians survey the first post-communist governments of the former Soviet Union, Gaidar's appointment will stand as either an extraordinary stroke of luck for Russia, or a reflection of Yeltsin's political genius. Price liberalization, massive defense cuts, and the initiation of privatization were truly extraordinary achievements in Russia at that time, and they occurred thanks to Gaidar.

Once Chernomyrdin assumed office, Gaidar's accomplishments appeared to be in grave danger. In early 1993, Chernomyrdin encouraged credits and subsidies to industry and agriculture, and engaged in virulent anti-privatization rhetoric, comparing it to Stalin's brutal collectivization of agriculture. He looked like the man the Parliament wanted. In response to continued challenges from Parliament, including a narrowly defeated vote to oust him, Yeltsin called for a referendum in April of 1993 on public support of him and his reforms. Thanks to Yeltsin's continued personal popularity and to intense popular disrespect for Parliament, 58 percent of the public endorsed the President and 53 percent upheld his reforms. The Parliament was discredited. Yet Yeltsin again failed to dissolve the Parliament and to call a new election. Inflation continued, since Chernomyrdin actively resisted the attempts to restrict the growth of credits made by Finance Minister Boris Fyodorov and Gaidar, who rejoined the government in September. In July, the Parliament renewed its attack on Yeltsin, but now privatization became a major target. The Parliament issued a series of resolutions declaring the end of privatization, each of which was reversed only a day later by presidential decree.

Finally, on September 21, after a series of blistering personal attacks against him, Yeltsin dissolved the Parliament and called a new parliamentary election for December. Rutskoi and Khasbulatov refused to end the parliamentary session, and on October 3 convinced their supporters to storm the Ostankino television station, starting a violent confrontation with the President. After a few days of uncertainty, the conflict ended as troops loyal to Yeltsin stormed the Parliament and captured its leaders, including the Speaker and the Vice President.

In anticipation of the December election, Gaidar formed a political party, Russia's Choice, of which he and Chubais became leaders. Russia's Choice ran on the platform of continuation of reforms, including privatization and stabilization. Perhaps surprisingly in light of the April referendum, Russia's Choice fared poorly after botching the campaign. The big winner was Vladimir Zhirinovsky, the ultra-nationalist advocate of a resurgent Russian empire. The communists and the agrarians also did very well. The outlook for reforms was poor, especially after both Gaidar and Fyodorov left the government in January. At the same time, the election delivered a new constitution that radically increased presidential powers. Despite all the turmoil, privatization had accelerated in the fall of 1993 largely because of the momentum generated by the popularity of vouchers.

In yet another twist of events, Prime Minister Chernomyrdin, his authority no longer challenged by Fyodorov, turned in favor of reforms in January of 1994. Assisted by the central bank governor Gerashchenko, he slowed down the growth of cheap credits to industry, though not to agriculture. Chernomyrdin also reversed his rhetoric against industrial privatization, and instead began talking about privatizing land.

The new Parliament focused its opposition to the government on political issues, such as freeing the instigators of the earlier parliamentary revolt. Moreover, Yeltsin now had a constitutional authority to rule by decree, which gave the government a relatively free hand in economic policy. In response to the tightening of credits, inflation fell sharply in 1994, reaching around 5 percent a month in August and September, although in October the ruble collapsed as inflation fears reemerged. Privatization continued to a triumphant completion in June, during which almost 3,000 firms were privatized. In fact, the Parliament came close to approving the next stage of privatization, which focused on cash sales of residual government shares and privatization of land, although eventually Chubais failed to get a majority and the program was passed by a Yeltsin decree. Relative to the previous two years, the first nine months of 1994 brought political peace and economic progress.

This brief history of Russian politics during this period hardly does justice to the drama and danger that surrounded the events. The President, the cabinet, and certainly the reforms appeared doomed on numerous occasions. It is all the more surprising, therefore, that privatization kept gaining ground through most of this period, so that, by the time relative political stability prevailed, most of the Russian economy was in private hands. How could this happen? In this book, we argue that the Russian privatization drew its momentum from the power of some key economic ideas.

2 Main Ideas

The people who put the Russian privatization program together shared three fundamental beliefs. None of these beliefs was particularly original, yet neither were they uncontroversial. In fact, much of the commonly espoused thinking about Russia, about economic reform, and about privatization directly opposed these beliefs.

Perhaps the one view that the Russian privatizers shared most strongly was that the Russian people, like the rest of the people in the world, were "economic men" who rationally responded to incentives. The privatizers rejected the widely held view that Russians were lacking in entrepreneurial ability, unusually suspicious of wealth and uninterested in working hard to become rich.

The belief in the preeminence of economic motives had some significant implications. It implied that, if only they were allowed, the Russian workers, managers, and the public at large would take advantage of the opportunity to become owners, and to invest their time and energy in getting rich. More radically, this idea implied that Russia did not need a third way of organizing its economic activity, such as market socialism or heavily regulated capitalism, to compensate for its alleged cultural specificities and deficiencies. On the contrary, this conviction that the Russians would rationally respond to economic incentives pointed to markets as the best way to organize economic activity in Russia, just as they are elsewhere in the world. In this respect, Russia is *not* different.

Although this belief was shared instinctively by the privatizers, there was some scientific basis for it as well. In two well-known articles, Robert Shiller, Maxim Boycko and Vladimir

Korobov presented the results of telephone surveys of individuals in several Russian, Ukrainian, East and West German, Japanese, and American cities.[1] All the respondents were asked the same set of questions about their attitudes toward markets. Shiller, Boycko, and Korobov discovered that the Russians and the Americans in particular held very similar views of private property and markets. Of course, many Russians were suspicious of capitalist institutions, but so were many Americans. In fact, they were about equally suspicious, suggesting that markets should work in Russia as badly, or as well, as they do in the West. The Shiller, Boycko, and Korobov papers dealt a powerful blow to the prejudice that "Russia is different."

Although the idea that the Russian people respond to economic incentives may seem obvious, it was by no means universally shared. Perhaps most importantly, virtually all Russian "reform" economists who came to prominence under Gorbachev, including Leonid Abalkin, Stanislav Shatalin, and Grigory Yavlinsky, believed that Russia was different, and rapidly turned into bitter enemies of Chubais's privatization. More surprisingly, the idea that the Russian people by their very nature are incapable of responding to incentives was shared by a group of scholars commonly known as Sovietologists, who built their careers studying the Soviet economic and political system. To them, a study such as that of Shiller, Boycko and Korobov simply must have been incorrectly designed or conducted, because it contradicted their image of the Russian people.[2] The experience of Russian privatization demonstrated how misguided the Gorbachev economists and Western Sovietologists were, and how clearly the Russian people revealed themselves as "economic men."

The second fundamental idea that the privatizers subscribed to was that, at least in Russia, political influence over economic life was the fundamental cause of economic inefficiency, and that the principal objective of reform was, therefore, to *depoliticize* economic life. Price liberalization fosters depoliticization because it deprives politicians of the opportunity to allocate goods. Privatization fosters depoliticization because it robs politicians of control over firms. When firms are subject to political influence, they cater to politicians by producing goods that consumers do not want, employing too many people, delivering output below cost to buyers favored by politicians and engaging in other grossly inefficient practices. Under socialism, firms were forced to pursue these political objectives, whereas during the Gorbachev transition, they pursued them in exchange for subsidies. The goal of privatization was to sever the links between enterprise managers and politicians, including both the Moscow industrial ministers and local officials, so as to force firms to cater to consumers and shareholders rather than politicians. There was no other way to achieve restructuring and efficient operation of firms. The three of us have elaborated the theme of depoliticization as a route to efficiency in several papers, and it will emerge as the principal theme of this book.[3] In retrospect, it is remarkable how clearly the privatizers agreed on the overwhelming need for depoliticization. To a large extent, Russian privatization succeeded because the privatizers focused on this primary objective and were prepared to compromise on less important issues.

Again, the idea that depoliticization is the principal goal of privatization was not entirely new. For example, British Chancellor of the Exchequer Nigel Lawson in his memoirs stated clearly that this was the principal objective of British privatization in the 1980s.[4] At the same time, many people believed, and still believe, that other objectives are as, or more, important. For example, many investment bankers, representatives of international lending agencies, and business people believed that Russian privatization should focus on selling firms one by one to substantial investors, especially foreign ones. Advocates of this view also often favored restructuring firms and even whole industries prior to privatization so as to prepare them for private ownership. The case-by-case method of privatization had an added advantage of generating revenue for the government. The Russian government, of course, badly needed cash. Thus to many Russians, as well as Westerners, case-by-case privatization appeared to be the right approach.

Nonetheless, if political influence is the main cause of inefficiency, then it is absurd to trust the ministries, or the investment bankers they designate, with finding foreign partners or with restructuring firms and entire industries. Russia's privatizers believed that politicians would use their power not to enhance efficiency, but to expand their economically undesirable control. As a result, the privatizers never seriously considered case-by-case privatization, and excluded those who advocated it too aggressively from the process. For example, the Russian State Committee on Foreign Investment was disbanded, its head shipped off to an honorific position in Washington, and the agency's advisors, the investment bank Goldman Sachs, left Russia for some time.

An alternative view, commonly articulated by academics working on privatization, stated that the goal of privatization should be to create a corporate governance system that would alleviate the conflicts of interest between managers and shareholders. In this view, privatization needs to solve the problem of managerial discretion rather than that of political discretion. The Russian privatizers tried hard to deal with this problem, but the goal of a better corporate governance system was clearly subordinate to that of depoliticization. In fact, the Russian privatizers paid a great deal of attention to Poland, where the focus on corporate governance gave rise to a privatization scheme in which firms were to be controlled by large, government-sponsored mutual funds.[5] This scheme was rejected for Russia precisely because of the expectation that any mutual fund created by the government would be politically influenced. It is worth noting that Polish privatization never got off the ground. Perhaps Russia avoided this failure by focusing on the right problem.

The third important idea shared by Russia's privatizers was that the Russian government did not really own the assets that needed to be privatized. In West European privatizations, the ruling governments, subject only to moderate political constraints, could dispose of public assets in any way they chose. Nigel Lawson, for example, makes it clear in his memoirs that the wide distribution of shares to the population that the British privatization achieved was an added political benefit but not an imperative. In Russia, in contrast, various "stakeholders," including the managers, the employees and the local governments, exercised substantial control over the allegedly public assets and could stop privatization if they chose to.[6] In return for their agreement to privatize, the stakeholders demanded significant payoffs. While the government owned the firms in the legal sense, it was not the sole owner in the sense of outright control over the decisions of firms, including the decision to privatize. In designing the program, the privatizers consistently and generously recognized stakeholders' claims, and thus ensured their eventual support of privatization.

At a theoretical level, the view of ownership as a system of control rights is derived from pathbreaking work by Sanford Grossman and Oliver Hart.[7] Their work was applied to privatization by Shleifer and Vishny at a conference in Cambridge in February of 1992, while the privatization program was being developed. The obvious implication of this view, namely the need to be generous to the employees and the managers to get privatization through, was not readily accepted in either Russia or the West, particularly by those who liked cash sales of firms to outsiders. Even some Russian reformers, such as Yavlinsky, bitterly criticized Chubais's privatization because of concerns with worker control. Ironically in light of this criticism, the greatest political threat to privatization came from those who wanted to give firms away lock, stock, and barrel to their "true owners," the employees and the managers, thereby creating closed companies like the traditional collective farms. The Russian privatizers found a middle road between the West European and the collective farm models, and thus avoided the problems of either extreme.

The three basic principles—that "economic man" is alive and well in Russia, that economic life must be depoliticized, and that the stakeholders already had substantial control rights in firms—shaped the Russian privatization program. The program's bottom-up approach relied extensively on a strong response from workers, managers, entrepreneurs and the public to the opportunities that privatization offered. Without a firm belief in the Russian citizen as homo economicus, this approach would not have made sense. Without a clear recognition that depoliticization was critical and that the enemy to be fought at all costs was the official bureaucracy, the program could have veered off in many directions. Lastly, without an appreciation that the claims of the stakeholders had to be respected, the program would have gone nowhere. In this book, we try to elaborate how these three ideas shaped the Russian privatization program and contributed to its success. In short, this book deals with ideas that worked.

3 Plan of the Book

Following this introduction, the book consists of five chapters and a conclusion. In chapter 2, we review the theory of ownership that focuses on the allocation of control rights over productive assets and rights to profits from these assets among various agents. We then go on to argue that political control over assets often represents an extremely inefficient ownership structure, which immediately leads to poor (politicized) resource allocation. The chapter concludes with a description of both traditional and latter-day socialism as manifestations of such inefficient ownership. To establish property rights, reforms must focus on depoliticization of economic activity.

Chapter 3 turns to alternative depoliticization strategies. It considers a variety of mechanisms for altering property rights in transition economies, including corruption, bureaucratic reform, nomenklatura privatization (politicians illegally assuming ownership), spontaneous privatization (managers illegally assuming ownership), and privatization proper (managers and investors legally assuming ownership). We argue that, from the viewpoints of both economic efficiency and political feasibility, privatization is the best strategy for achieving efficient ownership available to a free-market reformer. Chapter 3 makes the property rights case for privatization.

Chapter 4 turns to the design of the Russian privatization program given its principal goal of depoliticization and constraints arising from the pre-existing effective ownership structure. The chapter deals both with broad strategic decisions, such as the choice of mass rather than case-by-case privatization and the reliance on vouchers, and with fairly specific elements of program design, such as insider benefits and mechanisms of share sales. Chapter 4 shows how the broad ideas outlined above were translated into specific strategies and tactics of the privatization program.

Chapter 5 describes the results of Russian privatization, including the life story of the voucher. It offers the final statistics on its speed and breadth, but also describes the available evidence on the ownership structures of firms that emerged from privatization and the implications of these ownership structures for both depoliticization and corporate governance. Finally, chapter 5 presents evidence on the market values of assets during privatization and afterwards, and evaluates the effectiveness of privatization in light of this evidence.

Chapter 6 deals with restructuring that follows privatization, and proposes some policy steps to promote restructuring. In effect, it elaborates reform strategies aimed at promoting further depoliticization of the Russian economy. It deals with the formation of securities markets, real estate privatization, reform of the ownership of social assets, competition policy and other issues.

Chapter 7 concludes the book with a recapitulation of the main ideas, and how they worked in practice.

Notes

1. Robert J. Shiller, Maxim Boycko, and Vladimir Korobov (1991), "Popular Attitudes toward Free Markets: The Soviet Union and the United States Compared," *American Economic Review* 81, 385–400; and (1992), "Hunting for *Homo Sovieticus:* Situational versus Attitudinal Factors in Economic Behavior," *Brookings Papers on Economic Activity I,* 127–181.

2. Referring to Shiller, Boycko and Korobov (1991), *op.cit.,* Marshall I. Goldman writes: "It is hard to take such surveys seriously when the interviewing is done by telephone" (See *Lost Opportunity: Why Economic Reforms in Russia Have Not Worked,* New York: Norton, 1994, p. 18).

3. See Maxim Boycko, Andrei Shleifer and Robert W. Vishny (1993), "Privatizing Russia," *Brookings Papers on Economic Activity II,* 139–181; Boycko, Shleifer and Vishny (1994), "A Theory of Privatization," Harvard Institute of Economic Research, Working Paper No. 1689, August; and Shleifer and Vishny (1994), "Politicians and Firms," *Quarterly Journal of Economics,* CIX, 995–1025.

4. Nigel Lawson (1992), *The View from No. 11: Memoirs of a Tory Radical,* London: Bantam Press.

5. The intellectual case for the Polish approach is presented by David Lipton and Jeffrey D. Sachs (1990) in "Privatization in Eastern Europe: The Case of Poland," *Brookings Papers on Economic Activity II,* 293–341.

6. For an early discussion of the concept of stakeholders, see Andrei Shleifer and Lawrence H. Summers (1988), "Breach of Trust in Hostile Takeovers," in *Corporate Takeovers: Causes and Consequences,* ed. Alan J. Auerbach, Chicago: University of Chicago Press, 33–56.

7. Sanford J. Grossman and Oliver D. Hart, (1986), "The Costs and Benefits of Ownership: A Theory of Vertical and Lateral Integration," *Journal of Political Economy* 94, 691–719.

2

Political Control of Economic Activity

Economics attaches great importance to well-defined property rights as a determinant of economic success. When property rights over a productive asset are clearly specified, and the person who decides how to employ this asset bears full costs and enjoys full benefits of such employment, he puts the asset to its most productive use. This argument provides the ultimate rationale for relying on private property as the basis for an efficient organization of economic activity in a society. Prosperous economies—both contemporary and historic—succeed in establishing and maintaining well-functioning systems of private property rights.[1]

Conversely, it is commonplace to blame "poorly defined" property rights for bad economic performance, including that of communist Russia. Since our book deals with property rights, we begin this chapter with a characterization of the problem of "poorly defined property rights." We then show how political control of economic activity invariably causes this problem. Finally, we apply this analysis to Russia under both Soviet socialism and the Gorbachev transitional phase.

Like many other good things in economics, property rights analysis goes back to Adam Smith, who wrote that ". . . in all countries where there is tolerable security [of property], every man of common understanding will endeavor to employ whatever [capital] stock he can command. . . . A man must be perfectly crazy who, where there is tolerable security [of property], does not employ all the capital stock which he commands."[2] Two aspects of security of property have preoccupied economists and historians since (and before) Smith: protection of property and enforcement of contracts. Absence of police protection from expropriation by bandits, pirates, thieves, as well as feudal lords and other political "superiors" has deterred investment and growth throughout history.[3] Similarly, the inability to rely on courts to enforce agreements between private parties has slowed down commerce, which prevented the gains from trade so central to economic development from being realized. The lack of protection of property and of enforcement of contracts are the two very basic elements of poorly defined property rights.

An alternative, and complementary, view of poorly defined property rights associates them with the inefficiency of the underlying ownership structure. One example of inefficient ownership is the so-called separation of ownership and control in a public corporation, in which managers make decisions and shareholders bear the costs of these decisions. As a result, managers sometimes make decisions that benefit themselves rather than the shareholders.[4] Another example of inefficient ownership, as we show in this chapter, is state ownership. Inefficient ownership is as central to property rights analysis as the more traditional elements, such as contract enforcement.

In some cases, the consequences of inefficient ownership can be rectified with contracts that reward the decision maker for making an efficient decision. The result that ownership structure does not matter for the eventual outcome is known in economics as the Coase Theorem.[5] Importantly, for the Coase Theorem to work, property rights need to be protected and contracts need to be enforced. As we show in section 1, the Coase Theorem bridges the two elements of property rights analysis, since it shows that, for rights to be well defined, either a good system of property protection and contract enforcement are needed, or ownership structures must be efficient in the first place.

In section 2, we analyze a common instance of poorly defined property rights, namely the control of the use of productive assets by politicians. Political control fails both tests of well-defined property rights: the ownership structure entailed by political control is inefficient, and contracts cannot rectify this inefficiency legally, since such contracts usually involve bribes. For these reasons, poorly defined property rights are endemic when politicians control economic activity.

Some of the most telling evidence on the inefficiency of political control in market economies comes from the performance of state-owned enterprises in mixed economies. In section 3, we illustrate our view of the problems of political control using some of this evidence.

Nowhere was the problem of political control more clear than in communist Russia and other socialist countries. We believe that socialism is best described as a system of extreme political control of economic activity. In section 4, we describe the system of property rights under classical socialism, using the example of the Soviet Union. In section 5, we elaborate the evolution of this system in Russia under the Gorbachev regime. This enables us to discuss the inefficiency of property rights in a transition economy—a disease for which this book describes a cure.

1 Poorly Defined Property Rights

Consider a productive asset, such as a piece of land. Ownership rights to this asset are of two types: control rights and cash flow rights.[6] Control rights include all rights to make decisions on how to use the land: to grow vegetables or wheat, to turn it into pasture, to build an airport, or even to leave it idle. In addition, control rights include the rights to make transactions with the land: to lease it, sell it, or give it away. Cash flow rights are the rights to earn benefits and pay costs that result from a particular use of the asset. In the land example, the cash flow rights include the right to proceeds from selling vegetables, to rental income, and the obligation to pay real estate taxes.

In principle, there are many ways to allocate ownership rights to land among people. A farmer can have all the cash flow and control rights in full. Alternatively, a farmer can share ownership rights with his brother. For instance, the brother may have a right to 50 percent of the cash flows resulting from transactions with this piece of land, such as a sale or a lease, while the farmer has all the remaining control and cash flow rights (as was perhaps specified in their father's bequest). The structure of ownership rights is a distribution of rights among people.

The structure of ownership rights matters for how assets are used. Suppose that the farmer must choose between two alternative uses of land. He can either grow vegetables on the land, which brings a net income of $10,000 per year, or lease it to a rancher who can use it as pasture and is willing to pay rent of $15,000 per year. While ranching is the more profitable use for this land, the farmer cannot do it himself because he does not know how.

In the efficient world, the farmer possesses both control and cash flow rights to the land, and so prefers to rent it out and to enjoy $15,000 of net income. But consider two other possible scenarios. First, cash flow rights may be split, with rental income to be divided 50–50 between the farmer and his brother. In this case, the farmer is better off growing vegetables for $10,000 than collecting half of $15,000. Since he has all the control rights, he can make this choice.

Suppose alternatively that the farmer has all the cash flow rights, and is not required to share lease payments with his brother. He still has the choice between growing vegetables for a net income of $10,000 or leasing land for a net income of $15,000. However, his brother is the executor of their father's estate, which gives him some control rights. In this capacity he has to approve any transaction concerning family property, such as a lease. Would the farmer lease the land?

As before, the farmer would lease the land if he received all the income. However, the farmer recognizes that he needs his brother's approval for the lease, and the brother might demand a payment in return for his approval. In fact, the brother might ask for half of $15,000. If the brother actually does that, the farmer would rather stick to growing vegetables. The problem in this case is that, although cash flow rights reside completely with the farmer, control rights are split between him and his brother. The resulting ownership structure is inefficient.

The brother may seem implausibly heartless in this example, since he abuses his power of approval to extract money from a sibling. This objection surely has some validity when the two parties in a deal have blood ties, but what if the farmer needs to get the approval not from his brother but from an estate administrator he does not even know? In business transactions, there are multiple examples of such holdup problems, in which one party exploits its power to take advantage of another party. In one frequently discussed case, Fisher Body, the parts supplier to General Motors, sharply raised the price of its supplies when in 1926 GM wanted to buy more than Fisher Body agreed to make contractually. Because as an independent contractor Fisher Body controlled the supply decision, GM had to pay up. Eventually, GM bought Fisher Body, which meant that it now had the control rights and could tell its subsidiary what to supply and when. Such holdup problems resulting from split control rights are both common and serious.

The two examples illustrate two potential sources of inefficiency in the structure of ownership. The efficient structure is for a sole owner to make all decisions about the use of the land, and to pay all the costs and to earn all the benefits from such use.[7] The sole owner has full control rights and cash flow rights. In the examples, this is not the case. In the first example, the brother has some of the cash flow rights, and in the second he has some control rights. As a result, inefficient decisions are made. In these examples, establishing property rights amounts to moving to the case of a sole owner, who holds all control and cash flow rights.

Of course, as the Coase Theorem tells us, the farmer and his brother might be able to get around these inefficiencies. In the first example, the farmer and his brother can sign a contract according to which the brother gets only 20 percent of the lease income rather than the 50 percent he is entitled to in the will. If this happens, the farmer accepts $12,000 of lease income from ranching over the $10,000 from growing vegetables, whereas his brother gets $3,000 rather than nothing. Both are better off from this contract, and efficiency is restored. In the second example, for some fee, say $3,000, the brother may agree to relinquish his right to give approvals and to transfer this right to the farmer. With this piece of paper in hand, the farmer leases the land. Again, both the farmer and his brother are better off, and efficiency is restored.

The trouble is that Coasian contracting around inefficiencies requires an appropriate institutional structure.[8] To begin with, someone, such as the police, must protect the farmer's ownership rights to land, since if the land is subject to theft or expropriation no one would plant or lease it in the first place. Furthermore, when the brother agrees to take 20 percent, the courts must enforce the contract, for otherwise the brother could still demand his 50 percent of the net income. The fear of such a demand would make the farmer give up on the idea of leasing the land. Similarly, when the brother relinquishes his right to give approval, the contract must be enforceable in court to prevent the brother from changing his mind and still demanding half of $15,000. In particular, it must be possible to contract away the brother's approval right, for otherwise no court would enforce it. Again, the fear that the brother might still have the approval right could keep the farmer from leasing the land. The Coase Theorem shows how efficiency can be restored, but only if property is protected and contracts are enforced. This is done by functioning courts and police, which are the essential guardians of property and contracts when the ownership structure itself is not fully efficient.

To summarize, problems with property rights come from two sources: inefficiently distributed rights and inadequate institutions, which mean inadequate protection of rights and lack of contract enforcement. If cash flow and control rights were consolidated in one decision maker, he would presumably make an efficient decision. There are some exceptions to this rule but they are not critical for our analysis. Even if the ownership structure were inefficient, if rights were secure and all relevant contracts were enforceable, decision makers would bargain to an efficient outcome, and an inefficient ownership structure would not matter. The trouble is that, in real life, ownership structures are often inefficient *and* contracts getting around the inefficiency are not enforced. As the next two sections show, these dual problems are endemic to the case of political control of economic activity.

2 Political Control of Economic Activity

In many countries, the most serious problems with property rights result from political control of economic activity. In this section, we apply the theory of property rights outlined above to the case of political control.[9]

For concreteness, recall the second example of the previous section, in which the brother had to approve the lease of the land. Suppose instead that the lease must be approved not by the farmer's brother, but by a bureaucrat or a politician who approves all such transactions to protect the "public interest." In traditional economic analysis, the politician, as the servant of the people, would recognize that the efficient use of land is ranching, and would therefore promptly approve the lease.[10]

Unfortunately, many real world politicians do not act according to this public interest model, for three reasons. First, politicians usually do not have direct cash flow rights in the businesses subject to their control, and may simply not care about reaching an efficient decision. They certainly do not have a strong incentive to make the right decision. This would not be that serious if politicians were merely indifferent to the outcome, but becomes more serious in light of the next two problems.

Second, many politicians are subject to pressures from various interest groups, which do not represent the public interest, but rather the private interest of their constituencies. When politicians respond to campaign contributions and voting pressure from these well-organized interest groups, they are unlikely to serve the public interest, especially when the countervailing interest groups are not as well organized.[11] In these situations, politicians do not typically choose the efficient outcome, especially when they have no cash flow incentives.

Third, many politicians and bureaucrats, even when they are not subject to interest group pressure, have a concern with their own pockets. In exchange for an approval, such a politician might ask for a bribe. The person seeking the politician's approval can of course refuse to pay it, but then the politician might take months to ascertain which course of action best serves the poorly defined "public interest." To the extent that bureaucrats and politicians have some discretion, they have an opportunity to collect bribes. Corruption, of course, is pervasive in the world, though not in public finance textbooks. Coping with corruption can also reduce efficiency, and again the problem is worse when politicians have no stake in the efficient outcomes.

So what is the likely outcome when the farmer seeks the government approval for the lease? If the politician simply does not care about efficiency, he may or may not give the approval, depending on how he feels. But this politician may also be subject to pressure from the vegetarian lobby that opposes ranching, in which case he does care. If the meat lobby is not as well organized as the vegetarian lobby, the politician might refuse to approve the lease even if this outcome is efficient. Since the politician has no cash flow rights but has control rights, he can use them to further his political goals rather than to serve the public interest or efficiency. In this case, the farmer will stick to growing vegetables.

Even if the politician does not care about the vegetarian lobby, he may not grant his approval signature automatically. Just like the big brother in the previous section, he does not care if the land is used efficiently, and can refuse to approve its conversion, or delay granting his approval indefinitely, unless he is paid to do so. If the expected payment is half of $15,000, the farmer will grow vegetables. The efficient outcome is not attained.

But suppose the politician asks for a smaller bribe, say $3,000, so leasing the land is still attractive to the farmer. The trouble is that, unlike the brother from the earlier example, the politician cannot legally give up or sell his right of giving approvals, because doing so would conflict with his duty to serve the public interest. Because he cannot transfer the approval right legally, after collecting a bribe, the politician can always change his mind and refuse to allow the lease of the land, or claim that his superior overruled him. Unlike in the case of a contract between a farmer and his brother, the approval right is not transferable, and the bribe contract is not enforceable in court. We discuss this issue in more detail in chapter 3, but only note here that non-transferability of political control rights renders contracting around the inefficiencies much more difficult.

To make matters worse, unlike in the case of the farmer's brother, there are usually multiple politicians giving permits and approvals. To use the land for ranching, the farmer may need any number of permits from politicians overseeing water supply, fire safety, sanitation, land zoning, land leases, electricity supply, pollution control and so on. None of these politicians have legal cash flow rights in the farm, yet each can hold up the farmer for a payment in exchange for an approval. Moreover, for fear of being discovered, the politicians do not usually coordinate the bribes they request with each other, so the combined bribes they demand can easily exceed the value of the farm.

Split control rights between politicians are pervasive. In his fascinating account of small business in Peru, Hernando De Soto meticulously documented the dozens of permits and licenses that a small entrepreneur must obtain to start even a tiny proprietorship.[12] Since almost every bureaucrat that such an entrepreneur encounters demands a bribe, in the end it is usually cheaper not to get any permits at all and to stay in the informal sector. Again, the Coase Theorem does not help in getting around these problems when numerous politicians cannot legally coordinate their bribes.[13] The split of control rights between politicians makes the inefficiencies of political control much more difficult to get around than the non-political inefficiencies.

In sum, the inefficiency of political control is inherent in the very nature of rights that politicians have over productive assets. Politicians almost never have legal cash flow rights in these assets, and hence do not care about efficiency. Instead, politicians inherit their objectives from pressure groups that are not typically interested in value-maximizing use of assets. Politicians then cater to these pressure groups to stay in power or collect bribes. Finally, in most cases, the politicians' control rights are not legally transferable, which reduces the effectiveness of corruption even in the cases where it could increase efficiency. This problem is particularly severe in the case of multiple politicians with control rights over assets. In the rest of this chapter, we describe political control at work, and trace out its implications.

3 Public Enterprises

Perhaps the clearest evidence of the inefficiency of property rights structures in which politicians have substantial control rights comes from the analysis of public enterprises in modern mixed economies. Unlike in the case of regulated private businesses, in public enterprises cash flows belong to "the state," which usually means the Treasury. The bigger the losses of public enterprises, the less money the Treasury has to spend on other projects, including those that benefit the public, and the more taxes it has to raise. Conversely, the bigger the profits of public enterprises, the more money the Treasury has for projects and the lower are its needs for tax revenue.

While the cash flow rights belong to the Treasury, the control rights over a public enterprise are usually split between politicians, such as the ministers overseeing the enterprise, and the enterprise manager. The Treasury does not have any control rights, and the politicians again have no cash flow rights. In some cases, the manager has some cash flow rights because he is on an incentive contract tied to the profits of the enterprise. In practice, such incentive contracts are extremely uncommon, and, even in a few cases where they have been tried, politicians overseeing the enterprises have quickly repealed them once managers actually tried to maximize profits.[14] In sum, public enterprises exhibit all the key features of an inefficient ownership structure: the control rights are split between managers and various politicians, control rights are separated from cash flow rights (in fact, people with control rights have no cash flow rights), the politicians have objectives that need not coincide with efficiency, and the contracts designed to get around the inefficiencies (i.e., bribes) are not enforceable in courts.

In light of the theory, the evidence on the inefficiency of public enterprises is not surprising. The evidence shows that politicians use their control rights over these firms to force them to overemploy people, pay excess wages, locate in areas where it is not efficient to produce, and so on. For example, many state airlines, such as Greece's Olympic Airways and France's Air France, are notoriously overstaffed. "Operating costs at Europe's [state] airlines are 48 percent higher than at America's [private ones]," largely because of excess employment.[15] Some plants built by state companies, such as the Italian steel giant ILVA near Naples, never produce any goods and only put people on the payroll.[16] Public agencies providing municipal services in the United States typically employ 20 to 30 percent more people for a given output level than do private contractors.[17]

The beneficiaries of excess employment are often political supporters of the government, who value these jobs because they pay more than market wages. At public enterprises in Greece, many employees, and not just the top managers, turn over when an opposition party wins an election. In many American cities, such as Chicago, most city jobs are patronage jobs allocated to relatives and campaign activists. Public employees in local municipal services in the United States are both less productive than their private counterparts and better paid.[18]

Excess employment and wages in public enterprises are not the only sources of political benefits. Public enterprises in many cases produce goods desired by politicians rather than consumers. For example, the decision to produce the Concorde rather than a jetliner with a broader market appeal was made by French politicians despite the evidence that the demand for the Concorde would be low.[19] Credit Lyonnais, the giant French state bank, lost billions of dollars making dubious loans to friends of the socialist party.[20] Public enterprises are also frequently asked to locate their production in politically desirable rather than economically attractive regions. Thus Italian state firms are told to build production facilities in the South, the bedrock of support of the long-ruling Christian Democrats. Renault, Airbus Industries, Aeroports de Paris, all chose locations that pleased politicians rather than locations that minimized costs. These examples, of course, are only the tip of the iceberg of inefficiencies of public firms.

One might argue that these examples show that public enterprises pursue various social objectives, such as curing market failures or reducing inequality, rather than seeking a free market outcome. Theoretically, however, there is no reason to think that politicians cure market failures or reduce inequality. The strong special interest groups that the politicians cater to might in fact be the monopolies, or bad polluters. The politically influential groups in the population may be the rich, not the poor. Nor does the evidence support the argument that public control cures market failures and reduces inequality. For example, far from being more inclined to fight pollution, public firms are often the worst polluters, as the sad experience of Eastern Europe illustrates. Some public firms charge prices significantly below marginal cost to win political support, as the underpricing of railroad services in many European and Latin American countries and the cheap food policies in Africa show. In the case of food pricing in Africa, the beneficiaries are the relatively rich and politically active city residents, and the losers are the poor and politically inactive farmers.[21] Such pricing policies are strictly regressive, contrary to the view that public pricing redistributes income to the poor.

Most of the above examples are drawn from the experiences of mixed economies, in which the majority of economic activity originates in private firms, and only relatively little is done by public enterprises. While costly, the inefficiencies of public ownership do not disrupt the basic flow of private economic life. Put differently, the inefficient ownership structures of public firms are an exception, and the relatively efficient ownership structures of private firms are the rule, even though the private firms pay the cost of government regulation as well. Matters are quite different under socialism, where the basic inefficiency of the ownership structure is the same, but public control is much more pervasive. In addition, the objectives of the communist politicians are much more pernicious than those of the democratically elected socialists in mixed economies. In the next section, then, we describe what happens when public control dominates a nation's economy.

4 Ownership under Soviet Socialism

In an idealized textbook description, socialism is an economic system based on public ownership of productive assets. The so-called "state" allocates resources to maximize social welfare. To put this in the language of ownership rights, the state has the control rights, but also holds the cash flow rights on behalf of "the people." Because all control and cash flow rights are held together, the ownership structure, and hence the allocation of resources, is efficient.

An obvious problem with this description is that the state is actually a collection of politicians rather than a single entity. To describe socialism, we therefore have to be more specific about the ownership structure of assets: who has the cash flows and who has control rights over productive assets. Rather than dealing with theoretical models of socialism, we focus on the Soviet Union from the start.

In reality, there were three holders of property rights in a firm under Soviet socialism: the politicians, the managers, and the public. The essence of socialism was comprehensive political control over the economy. Specifically, the vast majority of control rights over productive assets under socialism was divided among various politicians, such as state bureaucrats and Communist party officials. To a much smaller degree, control rights were held by enterprise managers. Cash flow rights, in contrast, were firmly separated from both the politicians and the managers, and belonged to the public, which, as we argue below, paid for the politicians' decisions in terms of its living standards. Although, in theory, control and cash flow rights were held together by the socialist state, in practice there was a complete separation of those rights.

Most critical economic decisions under socialism were made by ministers and Communist party officials. We can debate the objectives of Communist party leadership, although few would argue, especially following Stalin's mass murders, that public welfare played much of a role. Instead, the communist objective was to build a powerful industrial state, with a huge army and police capable of defending the communist government from the threats of both external invasion and domestic unrest. To seek promotion, ministers and mid-level party officials pursued their specific versions of this objective, such as output increases or responsiveness to military needs. Communism thus built one of the world's most powerful war machines.

To pursue these objectives, the state bureaucracy controlled most of the economy down to many decisions at the firm level. Moscow officials decided what firms produced, where they got supplies, where they delivered the output, how many people they employed and at what wages, what investment and expansion projects firms would undertake, and what prices they could charge. A large number of government agencies controlled different aspects of these decisions, but their work was coordinated, and their control rights protected, by the Communist party, which served as the ultimate arbiter of all disputes. In this way, problems resulting from split control rights were minimized.

Under Soviet socialism, company managers played a secondary role. Their primary interest was the fulfillment of plans set out by the ministries and the growth of their enterprise. In fact, the great career success of an enterprise manager was to become a minister or a high-level party official himself, so that he could give orders to other managers. Of necessity, the managers had operating control over their enterprises, but these decision rights were minor compared to those of the managers in a market economy. Typically, managers lobbied the ministries for more help for their firms, and begged the suppliers for timely deliveries. Indeed, playing the system was one of the most valuable managerial skills under Soviet socialism. The bureaucrats made the major decisions, and used the Communist party to enforce them by making sure that the managers obeyed orders.

The official propaganda notwithstanding, workers had essentially no control rights under socialism. Their ability to strike for higher wages was held firmly in check, and the few spontaneous strikes that did occur were brutally suppressed. Similarly, local politicians were part of the central Communist party machine, and had vast control rights delegated to them from Moscow, but no independent source of authority. Leaders of the Communist party, and to a much smaller extent the managers and the local officials, shared control rights under socialism.

None of the parties with control rights, however, had any cash flow rights under socialism. As a result, none had any responsibility for the financial consequences of their decisions, or even could evaluate them given the prevailing price distortions. The cash flow rights under socialism were effectively held by the public. When the decisions of the ministries were economically wasteful, state firms lost money, though this was hard to measure because of distorted prices. When this happened, the public was taxed through lower real wages. If, in contrast, the decisions of the ministries created economic value, then the society grew richer and the government could afford to raise real living standards. Under Soviet socialism, the public as a whole paid for the efficiency or inefficiency of resource use determined by politicians.

The structure of ownership under Soviet socialism was thus both different from the textbook model and highly inefficient. The politicians had almost all the control rights, and no cash flow rights. The managers had some of the control rights, but no cash flow rights either. The objectives of the politicians who possessed the control rights were very far removed from the public interest. The virtually complete political control without countervailing cash flow rights to moderate political temptations did not constitute an efficient ownership structure. Even the countervailing influence of the voters, who in democratic countries sometimes rebel against the growth of the public sector and thus restrain the inefficiency of public firms, did not exist in the Soviet Union. The only efficient element of the Soviet ownership structure was that the Communist party coordinated political control, so it was hard for bureaucrats to operate at cross purposes. But even this element of efficiency was to disappear under Gorbachev.

Given this ownership structure, the allocation of resources under socialism was predictable. Communist party officials pursued vast and inefficient projects. Stalin carried these projects out most successfully by using slave labor. His successors had their own vastly inefficient programs as well. Nikita Khrushchev launched a Virgin Lands program designed to grow corn all over Siberia and Leonid Brezhnev started building the enormously expensive Baikal-Amur railroad through southern Siberia. Neither the politicians nor the managers cared about the cost of these projects, which was borne effectively by the public in the form of lower living standards. As a result, the socialist economy was characterized by tremendous waste and inefficiency, since cost control and maintenance received little or no priority. At the same time, military and industrial production continued to expand. The inefficiency of the structure of property rights caused a predictable inefficiency of resource allocation, but since the public did not vote its displeasure, and since, particularly in the 1970s and 1980s, oil revenues compensated for some of the political misdeeds, the system survived.

This analysis raises an interesting puzzle, namely, why did the communist leaders not translate their complete control rights into cash flow rights? In this case, they would have become, like Ferdinand Marcos of the Philippines, the real owners of the assets who could consume profits from the enterprises they controlled and who would therefore have been more interested in efficiency. To some extent, the communist leaders did translate their control rights into consumption, but only at the margin. They collected bribes in exchange for favors and through corruption assured themselves far greater wealth than the rest of the population. Still, this wealth was pitiful relative to that of capitalist dictators like Marcos or Mobutu Sese Seko of Zaire.

The reason that communist officials could not simply appropriate cash flows has mostly to do with official ideology, which gave them a mandate to govern and which they did not dare to ignore openly for fear of social unrest. It was simply too difficult, in most cases, for communist dictators to turn into capitalist dictators without risking a revolt. There may be a deeper explanation to this puzzle, but for now we simply continue to assume that the communist politicians received at best a trivial fraction of cash flow rights as individuals. The principal benefit of their control rights was the preservation of their comfortable jobs and living standards through the creation of a police state, which guaranteed both internal and external security.

5 Ownership under Gorbachev

The dramatic inefficiency of socialist production did not escape Russia's communist leaders. In response to the political need to improve living standards, over the decades they attempted a series of reforms. Unfortunately, these reforms sidestepped the fundamental problem of inefficient ownership, and thus often hurt rather than helped economic performance. Some of the most significant reforms were started by Gorbachev in 1986. These reforms maintained effective public ownership of cash flows, but reallocated the control rights from the Communist party to multiple uncoordinated government agencies as well as enterprise managers. The effect was predictable from theory: firms continued to be subject to intense, but now conflicting, political pressures, as well as demands for bribes by multiple bureaucrats and politicians.

A common idea behind many reforms was decentralization. Since the planners did not have access to all the information they needed to make efficient decisions, and themselves lacked incentives, the reforms allocated more control rights to enterprise managers, so that they could use their local knowledge to rationalize production and decrease waste. This reallocation of control rights from politicians to managers accelerated sharply under Gorbachev, who systematically transferred authority away from the ministries. During his tenure, Gorbachev stripped the ministries of their most important legal control rights, including the right to appoint managers, to establish production plans, and to allocate inputs. Yet the greatest reallocation of control rights occurred inadvertently with the demise of the Communist party, which had served as the principal mechanism of controlling managers. As the Communist party lost millions of members in 1990–91, and with them much of its coercive power, managers refused to obey instructions from Moscow.

The results of the reallocation of control rights from the politicians to the managers were predictable, though they did not evidently constitute an efficiency improvement. While the managers received many control rights, they still had no cash flow rights. Not surprisingly, they reacted to their new powers by trying to personally profit from them, and the most natural strategy was asset and output diversion. Specifically, a manager would use his independence to either sell output at low official prices with a large kick-back to himself, or to simply steal some of the enterprise assets and put them into a private company or cooperative that he controlled. These strategies disrupted the standard supply chains, since state firms could no longer count on deliveries from other state firms, which simply sold their products on the black market. Since only a few goods were allocated through the black market, however, these supply diversions did more to hurt the state sector than to help the private sector. Large state enterprises found their workers standing idle, lacking critical supplies that had been diverted to alternative use while other raw materials were rotting in their backyards.[22]

The collapse of the Communist party caused another key inefficiency of ownership under Gorbachev's socialism, namely the split of control rights among government agencies. Although Gorbachev transferred many control rights to the managers, the politicians remained extremely powerful, keeping control over export and import licenses, the allocation of critical inputs such as energy, and most important, government subsidies. Without the Communist party coordinating the activities of the various agencies, each one simply sought to expand its control over firms, and overlapping regulations proliferated rampantly. Every time a law was written in Russia, it circulated between various agencies of the government which were asked to comment. During 1991–92, each ministry introduced amendments that required its own approval of activities that the law regulated. If a law regulating joint ventures with foreign partners were considered, the finance ministry would insist on licensing joint ventures, the central bank would insist on licensing bank accounts of such ventures, the foreign trade authorities would want to control their imports and exports, the tax authority would demand a special jurisdiction, and so on.

Unlike under Soviet socialism, where the government bureaucrats used their control rights to further the aims of the Communist party and thus get promotions, the new bureaucrats lost that objective and simply sought bribes as well as new control rights to get still more bribes. Corruption became so extensive that many people thought it impossible to start a business in Russia. The split of political control among agencies with conflicting objectives after the collapse of the Communist party was probably as responsible for the economic decline during the transition from socialism to free markets as anything else.

Of the politicians who grabbed control rights from the center, none got more under Gorbachev, and subsequently Yeltsin, than local officials. Democratization led to the election of local officials with an independent source of political authority and hence control rights. The republics of the Soviet Union swiftly separated and the Union was dissolved. But even inside Russia itself, local politicians gained power independent of Moscow. In fact, to fight Gorbachev in 1991, Yeltsin appealed to local politicians to "take as much sovereignty as you can handle."

Local officials differed enormously, ranging from virulent nationalists in some ethnic parts of Russia, to hard-core communists in other regions, to traditional dictators in still others, to serious reformers in areas like Nizhny Novgorod, to corrupt machine politicians in the city of Moscow. Their political objectives were often very different from those of the central government bureaucrats, but not necessarily closer to efficiency. Moreover, the local officials now split control over local firms with the central government officials, and neither had any cash flow rights. The resulting ownership structure did not bode well for efficiency.

Whatever their political orientation, the local politicians have exercised their new control rights with a vengeance. They gained control over key local assets such as electrical, water and other utilities and used this control to influence local firms by renegotiating leases and threatening to cut off power. They often prevented the shipment of goods, especially consumer goods, out of their regions. They insisted on the right to participate in major ventures undertaken by local enterprises, particularly in the natural resource industries. Perhaps most importantly, however, they completely took over the regulation and control of small business from the central authorities. They used this control to pursue local political goals, as well as to receive payoffs for themselves. Local corruption in Russia increased even more than federal corruption.

Although less noticeably than the managers and the local officials, enterprise employees also gained some control rights given up by the Communist party. At the enterprises, they had some formal, though weak, voice in appointing managers. More importantly, as the Communist party ceded its monopoly on political power, politicians catering to worker interests gained power in the Parliament, which gave workers an important voice through the political process. Once privatization was undertaken in 1992, this voice was increasingly heard.

In sum, the ownership structure under Soviet socialism was characterized by a number of fundamental inefficiencies, the most conspicuous of which was the separation of cash flow and control rights. The ownership reform under Gorbachev did not move toward greater efficiency, and in many ways made matters worse. Managers obtained a lot of control rights and no cash flow rights, which greatly stimulated theft without necessarily stimulating efficiency improvements. The Communist party lost its control rights, but these rights were split between many agencies acting essentially independently, including most conspicuously the local governments. As a result, firms faced continued pressure to pursue political objectives, except now, more often than not, these objectives conflicted with each other. In addition, corruption increased tremendously as managers were fleeced by more and more officials with control rights over firms. From the ownership perspective, the Russian economic predicament at the turn of the decade was not entirely surprising.

Nor did the collapse of socialism brighten the near-term outlook for property protection and contract enforcement. Under socialism, contracts between private entities did not play a large role, and the Communist party enforced agreements between government entities. As the Communist party collapsed, this approach to enforcing agreements collapsed as well without being replaced by an alternative enforcement system. At the same time, the protection of property by police deteriorated as well in part because the control of police and the KGB by the Communist party vanished without being replaced by effective local political control.

Unconstrained by the Communist party, many government agencies vastly expanded the scope of their regulatory control, often at odds with the control rights of other agencies. At the same time, as the opportunities for private business expanded in 1992 and 1993, the demand for both protection of private property and private contract enforcement increased sharply. Since this increase in demand was not met by the supply of these services by the government, the private sector filled in the gap, often imperfectly, with mafia-style protection organizations. The Gorbachev transition thus left Russia not only with a highly inefficient ownership structure, but also with a virtual absence of institutions allowing for contracting around the inefficiencies.

The economic pathologies of the transition period raise the central question in this book, namely, how to transform the ownership structures emerging during late socialism into efficient ones? In chapter 3, we evaluate alternative strategies of addressing the problem of inefficient ownership structures resulting from excessive political influence. In the subsequent chapters, we apply the theory developed in this chapter and the next to the experience of the Russian privatization.

Notes

1. The best works on property rights include Adam Smith (1776) [1976], *The Wealth of Nations,* Chicago: University of Chicago Press; Douglass C. North (1981), *Structure and Change in Economic History,* New York: Norton; Yoram Barzel (1989) *Economic Analysis of Property Rights,* Cambridge: University Press; and Mancur Olson (1982), *The Rise and Decline of Nations,* New Haven: Yale University Press.

2. Adam Smith, *op.cit.,* cited in J. Bradford De Long and Andrei Shleifer (1993), "Princes and Merchants: European City Growth Before the Industrial Revolution," *Journal of Law and Economics* XXXVI, 671.

3. For evidence, see North, *op.cit.,* and De Long and Shleifer, *op.cit,* 671–702.

4. On this agency problem, see Adolf A. Berle and Gardiner C. Means (1932), *The Modern Corporation and Private Property,* New York: Macmillan; and Michael C. Jensen and William H. Meckling (1976), "Theory of the Firm: Managerial Behavior, Agency Costs and the Ownership Structure," *Journal of Financial Economics* 3, 305–360.

5. Ronald H. Coase (1960), "The Problem of Social Cost," *Journal of Law and Economics* 3, 1–44.

6. The distinction between cash flow and control rights, as well as the foundations of the analysis that follows, are due to Sanford J. Grossman and Oliver D. Hart (1986), "The Costs and Benefits of Ownership: A Theory of Vertical and Lateral Integration," *Journal of Political Economy* 94, 691–719; and Oliver D. Hart and John Moore (1990), "Property Rights and the Nature of the Firm," *Journal of Political Economy* 98, 1119–1158.

7. Some exceptions to this rule are discussed in Grossman and Hart, *op.cit.*

8. An additional problem, stressed by Grossman and Hart, *op.cit.*, is that future contingencies may be difficult to describe and therefore contracts are inherently incomplete. While this is clearly important, some of the contracting difficulties central to our analysis, such as lack of contract enforcement, are even more basic.

9. This section draws on Maxim Boycko, Andrei Shleifer and Robert W. Vishny (1993), "Privatizing Russia,"*Brookings Papers on Economic Activity II,* 139–181; and Andrei Shleifer and Robert W. Vishny (1994), "Politicians and Firms," *The Quarterly Journal of Economics* CIX, 995–1025.

10. The classic reference is Richard A. Musgrave (1959), *The Theory of Public Finance,* New York: McGraw-Hill.

11. Mancur Olson (1965), *The Logic of Collective Action,* Cambridge: Harvard University Press.

12. Hernando De Soto (1989), *The Other Path,* New York: Harper and Row.

13. For an analysis of this problem, see Andrei Shleifer and Robert W. Vishny (1993), "Corruption," *The Quarterly Journal of Economics* CVIII, 599–617.

14. This observation is documented in John Nellis (1988), "Contract Plans and Public Enterprise Performance," World Bank Staff Working Paper No. 118.

15. *The Economist,* "European Airlines: Flights of Fancy," CCCXXX (February 5, 1994), 69–70.

16. *The Economist,* "Two Half Revolutions" CCCXXX (January 22, 1994), 55–58.

17. John D. Donahue (1989), *The Privatization Decision,* New York: Basic Books.

18. Donahue, *op.cit.*

19. Jean-Pierre C. Anastassopoulos (1981), "The French Experience: Conflicts with Government," in Raymond Vernon and Yair Aharoni, eds., *State-owned Enterprise in the Western Economies,* London: Croom Helm, 99–116.

20. *The Economist,* "The Bank That Couldn't Say No," CCCXXXI (April 9, 1994), 21–24.

21. Robert Bates (1981), *Markets and States in Tropical Africa: The Political Basis of Agricultural Policies,* Berkeley: University of California Press.

22. This argument is elaborated in Kevin M. Murphy, Andrei Shleifer and Robert W. Vishny (1992), "The Transition to a Market Economy: Pitfalls of Partial Reform," *Quarterly Journal of Economics* CVII, 889–906.

3

Paths to Efficient Ownership

The previous chapter described the ownership structure of firms through the last days of Soviet socialism. The cash flows of these firms belonged to the public, while control was split between their managers and the numerous politicians (or bureaucrats) overseeing them. Generally, efficient ownership requires that control rights and cash flow rights over an asset be held in tandem by a decision maker whose interests are aligned with efficiency. The ownership of firms during the last days of socialism was therefore far from efficient, which lead to economic stagnation. To turn the economy around, free-market reformers had to create efficient ownership. In this chapter, we examine the range of available paths to that goal.

The first question we must face, however, is who are these market reformers? There have been quite a few market reformers around the world in recent years, including Margaret Thatcher of Britain, Carlos Salinas de Gortari of Mexico, Leszek Balcerowicz of Poland, Vaclav Klaus of the Czech Republic, Gaidar and Chubais of Russia, not to mention free-market dictators such as Augusto Pinochet of Chile. All of them oversaw a massive retreat of government from economic activity. What do they all have in common?

We believe that the free-market reformers are politicians whose political constituency is the productive part of the economy, and whose political enemies represent the unproductive part. In the West, free-market reformers often are leaders of tax revolts, and their backers are economically productive members of the society opposed to being overtaxed. Their opponents, in contrast, are public sector employees and welfare recipients who benefit from government spending. In Russia (and Eastern Europe), free-market reformers tend to represent a newly formed political coalition comprised of entrepreneurs, professionals, small business people, professionals, and other property owners. Their opponents, who most frequently are the communists and the nationalists, represent the employees of the declining state firms and collective farms, the military, pensioners and others who benefit from government largesse.

Around the world, free-market reformers often hold the position of finance minister or head of the Treasury. Since the Treasury collects the taxes and pays for the government's expenditures, it effectively holds the public cash flow rights in state firms. When state firms lose money and the Treasury subsidizes them, it needs to tax the economically productive parts of the economy. When state firms make money, the Treasury can afford to tax the productive parts of the economy less. Not surprisingly, entrenched politicians want the Treasury to spend more money, and to collect higher taxes from the productive parts of the economy to spend on state firms. In contrast, entrepreneurs and professionals want the Treasury to spend less and tax them less. Since the free-market reformer represents the latter, he often needs to control the Treasury to combat the entrenched politicians. Because privatization undercuts these politicians, the Treasury typically serves as the government agency in charge of privatization.

Being a free-market reformer also requires some appreciation of basic economic principles, such as that people respond to incentives. Not every politician is therefore capable of becoming a reformer. Without his belief in the Russian individual as homo economicus, Chubais could not have had the confidence to carry out his privatization program.

Reformers need not be any more committed to the "public interest" than the communists. For example, Prime Minister Chernomyrdin has pursued more successful stabilization policies than Gaidar, in part because the energy sector of the Russian economy, which was the backbone of Chernomyrdin's political base, did not want unproductive industry and agriculture to be subsidized at its expense. Other reformers, too, have their political allies. Nonetheless, the fundamental point is that, starting from an overpoliticized economy, the policies that reformers pursue to serve their personal political goals are much closer to the public interest than the policies of the anti-reformers interested in a powerful state. From the vantage point of Gorbachev's Russia, Sweden and the United States were virtually indistinguishable. To get to either destination, a vast retrenchment of the government from economic life had to be accomplished. Whatever his ultimate political interest, a free-market reformer had to aspire to that goal.

Several alternative paths are open to a free-market reformer pursuing efficient ownership. The first path is to do nothing and let managers and politicians negotiate to the efficient outcome, as the Coase Theorem says they should. The second path is to consolidate control rights in the hands of a public-spirited bureaucracy. The third path, known as nomenklatura privatization, is to have politicians both control firms and receive their profits. The fourth path is to concentrate both control rights and cash flow rights in the hands of the managers (and outside investors). One way to do this is to simply permit spontaneous privatization, in which managers steal assets to obtain both cash flow and control rights. Alternatively, the reformer can change laws so as to legitimately take control rights from politicians. The allocation to the managers of control rights that once belonged to politicians is known as corporatization; the allocation to them, as well as to outside investors, of cash flow rights is known as privatization. The principal conclusion of this chapter is that the combination of corporatization and privatization is the only politically viable strategy for creating efficient ownership.

Anti-reformist politicians do not appreciate having control rights seized from them and given to the managers. In fact, they resist fiercely. As a result, viable privatization strategies require building political coalitions that remove control rights from traditional politicians. These coalitions are usually created by giving some cash flow ownership to parties other than the management, including employees and most importantly the public. The various stakeholders in the coalition are thus persuaded to back privatization. As a result, privatized firms become owned by their managers, employees, and outside shareholders.

Is this ownership structure efficient? Not completely. Even after firms are privatized, politicians attempt to influence them through regulations and subsidies, so privatization by itself does not entirely take the government out of economic activity. Moreover, outside investors end up with cash flow rights but often not much real control, which enables managers to pursue self-serving inefficient policies at shareholders' expense. Toward the end of this chapter, we briefly discuss the road to efficient ownership beyond privatization.

1 Corruption

The easiest depoliticization strategy is to do nothing, and let politicians and managers sort out the inefficiencies between themselves. To some extent, this happens anyway. After all, in the pure Coasian world, there is no problem with the inefficiently split ownership rights. For example, suppose that a bureaucrat can shut down a business because it allegedly violates the fire code. If it is efficient for the business to operate, the bureaucrat and the manager simply negotiate to this outcome. Put differently, the manager bribes the bureaucrat to permit him to operate. One can argue, of course, that if the manager always needs to bribe some bureaucrat, he does not invest in his business for fear of expropriation, which leads to another inefficiency. But an extended Coasian argument applies to such investments as well. Just as the bureaucrat sells his right to close the business, he also sells the right to any future interference, which gives the manager correct investment incentives.[1] The word corruption is not used pejoratively in this analysis. Corruption is no different from any other side payment in the Coase Theorem.[2]

Corruption is so routine in transition economies that it is almost unnecessary to give examples. Many politicians take bribes in exchange for their signatures, and almost everything requires signatures of politicians. Many high-ranking bureaucrats in Russia actually refer the seekers of their signatures to specialized consulting firms, of which they are often part-owners and which for a fee prepare documents in a format that the bureaucrat finds easy to read and sign. The Coase Theorem is hard at work.

So, what's wrong with corruption? One problem is that it may not work because corruption "contracts" are not enforceable in court. The arbitrary element of a politician's control rights, which enables him to collect bribes, does not constitute a legal right that a court would protect or that he can surrender through a contract enforceable in court. In practice this means that the politician can come back and demand another bribe from the manager, or another politician can also demand a bribe. The problem of having to bribe everybody, and of not being assured of getting what one has paid for, has plagued every businessman, domestic or foreign, operating in today's Russia. But without enforceable contracts, corruption is ineffective in neutralizing political control.

Courts, of course, are not the only mechanism for contract enforcement. In some cases, reputation is an alternative. For example, in some East Asian countries, governing parties allegedly maintain a reputation for moderate corruption, and enforce the bribe contracts. A manager pays a small bribe to a local official to do what he wants. If the official demands a higher bribe, the deviation becomes known to his superiors, and the official is replaced. But in Russia and other transition economies, the horizons of individual politicians are too short and political parties are too weak to sustain corruption contracts through reputation. Similarly, organized violence is a potential enforcement strategy, although it is typically used to address breach of contract by private parties rather than by politicians. Even in Russia, politicians are only rarely shot. In sum, when the bribe contract enforcement fails, managers do not pay bribes to get control rights, and the split property rights problem is not resolved.

If unenforceability of corruption contracts is such a big problem, why doesn't a free-market reformer hunker down and enforce corruption contracts? There are at least three reasons. First, political control rights are necessarily split, and bribing one politician does not assure cooperation from another. Persuading all politicians with control rights to participate simultaneously in one grand Coasian bargain may be impossible, since some can always hold out. In Russia, documents pertaining to important enterprises often require a dozen signatures, which in turn call for too many bribes for these documents to ever be approved. The split of control rights among politicians sharply reduces the effectiveness of corruption as a means of dealing with inefficient ownership structures.

Second, even if corruption addresses the problem of split control rights, it does not produce efficient ownership if cash flows remain public, and so cash flow and control rights are not aligned. In many cases, managers bribe politicians to help them steal public assets or to find ways to avoid remitting profits to the Treasury. For example, bribing politicians is usually an integral part of spontaneous privatization of assets. Bribes are also an essential element of tax evasion. These strategies are often highly inefficient: it is common to see public firms in Russia shutting down simply because some machines or inputs have been diverted by the managers who bribed politicians to let them do so.

Third, and perhaps most important, enforcing corruption contracts only encourages politicians to generate new control rights for themselves, which would of course eventually stop all business. Because in a developing or a transition economy many legal control rights are neither spelled out nor enforced, these rights are in danger of being grabbed by the politicians. If a person does not have a full legal right to occupy a piece of land, he is in constant danger of being kicked off by a politician or a bureaucrat who claims a "public" right to that land. If corruption contracts were enforceable, all land would end up condemned by politicians, a clearly unappealing outcome.

A good illustration of this principle comes from the Russian State Anti-Monopoly Committee, which was assigned the task of regulating monopolies in Russia. Not surprisingly, in response to being charged with this task, the Committee compiled a list of *thousands* of firms in Russia that it classified as monopolies. A few dozen national monopolies were included, but so were local bakeries, bathhouses, etc. Firms immediately started bribing local anti-monopoly officials just to get off the list! If corruption contracts were enforceable, every firm in Russia would have become a monopoly under a suitable market definition.

An equally good illustration comes from the bankruptcy law recently introduced in Russia. Having listened to some Western advisors on the relative merits of rehabilitation and liquidation of bankrupt firms, the agency responsible for creating a bankruptcy procedure arrived at the following solution. The agency assigned to itself the task of deciding which firms were bankrupt, and in fact maintained a list of bankrupt firms. Once the agency declared a firm bankrupt on the basis of some criteria it had developed, the relevant bureaucrat would consider whether to liquidate the firm, or to allocate government subsidies to rehabilitate it. The creditors and the management would not have any formal voice in this decision, although the bureaucrat would of course appreciate their intellectual as well as other, more tangible, contributions to the decision.

The bottom line is that corruption does not solve efficiency problems, and often makes matters worse. In fact, we believe that the problems with corruption we have just outlined make it a huge burden on the Russian economy. Not surprisingly, therefore, corruption in Russia and elsewhere has been extremely unpopular. Perhaps in part for this reason, no reformer has relied on corruption in solving the ownership problem.

2 Reforming Bureaucracy

If the reformer really decides to reform, perhaps the ideal approach to aligning cash flow and control rights of firms in a transition economy is to give control back to the public, as represented by benevolent bureaucrats and politicians. This strategy is often advocated in the context of transition economies by socialists as well as students of the East Asian growth miracle.[3] The basic idea is for a reformer to create a new government bureaucracy that, unlike the old politicians serving vested interests, is both efficient and public-spirited. With such a bureaucracy, cash flows can remain public, and control rights will be exercised to serve the public as well.

Experience reveals some, but not many, episodes of powerful and efficient bureaucracies, although their public spiritedness is less evident. Examples include the Korean bureaucracy after the 1961 coup, some local governments, such as that in West Bengal in India, the United States Forest Service in the first half of this century, and arguably some parts of the French civil service, although the latter recently has been discredited by scandals.

Such effective bureaucracies appear under rather special circumstances. Sometimes they appear in military dictatorships (Korea, Taiwan) or in non-military dictatorships (Singapore), where the boss can seriously harm ineffective subordinates. The military dictators in these cases succeed in generating rapid economic growth, although their true objective might be a military build-up rather than national prosperity. Interestingly, some of the most efficient public enterprises in East Asia have been run by generals directly subordinate to dictators.

Effective bureaucracies also occasionally appear at the local level, where free press and the electorate closely monitor the politicians, as in the case of some local governments in the United States. In these situations, politicians truly become agents of the public, since deviations from such behavior quickly become exposed and electorally penalized. In discussing such instances, we should remember how rare they are even in advanced democratic countries.

Lastly, in some cases politicians decide to serve the public interest under the influence of ideology. For example, the communist local government in West Bengal efficiently provides many public services allegedly because it believes in public service and not just re-election. The idea of public service has also apparently influenced the dictators in East Asia. One should not push these examples too far, however. Ideological politicians are sometimes mistaken about public interest or even psychologically imbalanced, as the examples of Benito Mussolini or the FBI's J. Edgar Hoover illustrate. Nor is the record of socialist dictators proclaiming their service to the public encouraging in this regard. Even the best of the East Asian dictators, such as Singapore's Lee Kuan Yew, have recently been criticized for generating growth through low consumption and high capital accumulation rather than through productivity gains.[4] Ideology is at best a risky route to serving the public interest.

In sum, the idea of creating an effective, public-spirited bureaucracy as a way to align cash flow and control rights over firms is more attractive in theory than in practice. We are deeply skeptical that such bureaucracies can be created in Russia any time soon. Those politicians standing ready to assume absolute power in Russia at the moment look far from benevolent. At the same time, democratic institutions are not sufficiently developed to provide the close monitoring that would force civic mindedness on the politicians. Many local political machines are controlled by the old communists, and the press is often bought off. Finally, if bureaucrats in Russia have any true ideology, it is that of enriching themselves. Creating an ideological bureaucracy would require either eliminating the existing bureaucrats (which is sometimes done in revolutions), or replacing most of them (as has been done in some East European countries). Russia has not done either. As a result, not only cannot a reformer count on ideologically motivated, public-spirited bureaucrats any time soon, but he must also put up with tremendous resistance to change from the traditional bureaucrats.

3 Politicians as Owners

If the public cannot regain control over assets, the reformer has to turn either politicians or managers into owners. In one approach to this problem, communist politicians in Eastern Europe and Russia have advocated the consolidation of political control and the return to classical socialism. The stated motivation behind these strategies is to restore production by rebuilding links between enterprises through central coordination. A memorandum circulated by one of the Russian ministries in early 1992 stressed the importance of vertical integration of production through central control to avoid the vagaries of the market, and cited the authority of Ronald Coase in support! The mechanism for implementing these strategies was to recreate sectoral ministries, often under new names like "industrial associations." Through these institutions, traditional politicians hoped to regain control over firms from enterprise managers.

The return to political control of assets while cash flows remain public does not improve efficiency. As we argued in chapter 2, this ownership structure is responsible for the extraordinary inefficiency of socialist production in the first place, since politicians did not have to pay for catering to their interest groups. Even if the politicians restored old production levels through remilitarization of the economy, the public would lose. Indeed, while much of the decline of production in Eastern Europe and Russia during reforms has reflected the collapse of the military sector, that decline has been accompanied by growth in private consumption. The return of control rights to the politicians would consolidate control rights, but would still reduce efficiency both because cash flows remain separated from control rights and because politicians have bad objectives.

The more comprehensive approach to turning politicians into owners is to give them both control and cash flow rights. Cash flow rights are usually transferred to a politician under the guise of some legal procedure, although both the letter and the spirit of the law are typically overlooked. Sometimes the transfer takes the form of privatization where the winner is rigged to be the politician or his relative. In some developing countries, privatization takes the form of selling public firms to the relatives of the top politicians, their allies, and important generals. In Russia, similar deals are called nomenklatura privatization. In some cases, a new company jointly owned by the government and the politician as a private person is formed, to which the government contributes factories and other property, and the politician contributes his management skills. In other cases, a politician and a manager simply steal some state assets and put them into a private firm they jointly own.

The structure of ownership emerging from nomenklatura privatization is arguably more efficient than that with public ownership of cash flows. The politician may still pursue goals other than value maximization, but now he bears the cost of the inefficiencies he imposes, and hence demands that there be fewer of them. In our earlier example of the bureaucrat enforcing the fire code, he is unlikely to find a business in violation when he owns the business himself. Nonetheless, nomenklatura privatization does not achieve full depoliticization (and efficient ownership) unless politicians retire from office, since their objectives continue to give weight to interest groups that support them. In addition, nomenklatura privatization has major political problems. Giving politicians equity is obviously extremely unfair, which is presumably why the transfer of these claims to politicians usually occurs semi-legally. Like corruption, nomenklatura privatization rewards arbitrary grabbing of control rights and openly acknowledges that politicians are not acting in the public interest. For this reason, few governments have openly subscribed to nomenklatura privatization.

Moreover, entrenching old politicians as shareholders, while giving them good incentives, reduces the likelihood that control over assets will shift to managers with skills needed to restructure firms. These politicians are good at designing subsidy programs, not business plans. To the extent that management turnover is essential for efficient resource allocation, giving equity to the politicians can entrench the old human capital and thereby reduce efficiency.

In the end, nomenklatura privatization is not a viable option for a reformer. It fails to depoliticize firms, and it helps the reformer's enemies rather than his supporters.

4 Managers as Owners

If the reformer does not pursue ownership by politicians, he has to turn to managers. One approach is to let managers appropriate the assets, so that they simultaneously obtain cash flow rights and escape political control. In Russia and elsewhere, this strategy is referred to as spontaneous privatization, and has been practiced to some extent through diversion of assets to private companies. In 1991–92, it was common for a firm to sell so-called surplus assets, or even final output, at a discount to a company privately owned by the manager. Once this process is complete, managers effectively become full owners. Of course, politicians do not like the loss of control and income they experience, and hence oppose such spontaneous privatization. In fact, this opposition is part of the platform of communist parties in most countries in Eastern Europe. Nor is the public usually happy about the massive theft of public assets. Politically, then, spontaneous privatization is extremely costly to reformers.

A more effective strategy of turning managers into owners is through legal reform. To begin, the reformer must take away from the politicians their legal means of protecting their control rights. After all, politicians only have control rights over assets because laws on the books entitle them to these rights, and the police and the courts enforce them. A reformer can try to change these laws, and reallocate control from politicians to managers. The principal form of this reallocation is called corporatization (or commercialization), which basically refers to the transfer of control rights from ministers to managers. This can happen in a variety of ways. In Poland, public enterprises changed their formal governance structure from ministerial oversight to that by boards of directors with managers, workers, and ministries all represented. In Russia, the process was more informal, with the Gorbachev, and subsequently Yeltsin, administrations depriving the ministries of their traditional control mechanisms. As a result, control rights, including the dominance of the boards of directors, devolved to managers. The differences between countries should not, however, distract from the fundamental fact that corporatization transfers control rights from politicians to managers.

Following corporatization, efficient ownership demands that cash flow rights be allocated from the Treasury. This transfer, known as privatization, can take a variety of forms, but usually involves either a sale or a subsidized hand-over of cash flow rights to the managers as well as other investors who share control rights with them. Privatization brings the manager a legal, secure, and transferable cash flow claim. Now both cash flow and control rights are consolidated in the managers' hands and, since managers do not have to cater to interest groups, they are likely to respond to having both cash flow and control rights by maximizing profits.

It is useful to think of corporatization and privatization as separate steps, although they are often administratively combined. When shares in firms have both cash flow rights and votes attached to them, the transfer of the majority of shares to private parties accomplishes privatization and corporatization simultaneously. Nonetheless, corporatization can take place without privatization. In Poland, managers received much freedom from the ministries while firms remained publicly owned. Privatization of cash flows can also occur without corporatization, if, for example, politicians continue heavy regulation of privatized firms. Many Russian firms, particularly in the natural resource sector, are headed in this direction. The difference between corporatization and privatization is of some historical significance as well, as we point out below.

In our simple framework, turning managers into owners is the most appealing path to achieving an efficient ownership structure. But this path raises two key questions. First, is this approach feasible from a political viewpoint? Second, does this approach really achieve efficient ownership? Answers to both questions are complicated, since the managers, the politicians and the Treasury are not the only players in the game.

5 Hurdles

барьер

The privatization model outlined above omits important political and economic factors. The stark picture of the public, politicians and managers as the only parties with potential cash flow and control rights ignores other stakeholders who have significant ownership rights in public assets. In many countries, for instance, workers' collectives have substantial ownership rights. In Poland, workers' councils played a key formal role in enterprise decision making after Solidarity assumed power. In addition, labor unions had a lot of influence over economic policy. In Russia, with the exception of a few industries such as coal, unions had much less formal authority in the enterprises, and in most cases were controlled by managers. However, as voters and as a reasonably well-organized interest group, workers' collectives exercised a great deal of influence over the reallocation of ownership.

In addition, regional governments often play an important role in controlling firms through local regulations. Regional differences created vastly different privatization programs in the Czech and Slovak Republics, for example, because the government of Slovakia, with a high concentration of military industry, had little interest in depoliticization. Ultimately, these differences may have contributed to the split-up of Czechoslovakia. In Russia, a number of powerful regional governments, such as those in Tatarstan and in the city of Moscow, developed their own privatization programs, reflecting the different political goals of the respective governments. All over Russia, local politicians obtained enormous control rights that could not be ignored.

For privatization to work politically, a reformer cannot simply give firms to managers without addressing the demands of the other stakeholders. Nor can he legitimately ignore voter opposition to a straight transfer of public cash flows to a few managers. Moreover, politicians in all countries resist the alienation of their control rights, since they suffer large wealth losses when their corruption income is eroded. In Russia, both local and national politicians opposed privatization. At the national level, for example, the minister of publishing demanded that all publishing houses remain in state hands because "publishing is our ideology," and hence cannot be given up to the private sector. The construction minister insisted that all trucks must remain in state hands because they would be needed in a war mobilization effort. Most industries, in one way or another, served national security. At the local level, politicians in some parts of Russia have succeeded in blocking privatization, and in other parts distorted it beyond recognition, citing the need to protect regional independence.

A feasible privatization program must therefore remove control rights from the politicians by enlisting the support of the other stakeholders and the public. This requires building a political coalition with the managers, the workers, the regional governments, and the public in general. In the case of privatization, this coalition is sometimes easier to build than in other reforms, since the reformer has the Treasury's formal cash flow rights to give away. Our discussion of the Russian privatization model in chapter 4 is largely the story of such coalition building.

From the viewpoint of efficient ownership, turning managers into owners is not the end of the story either. It is by no means certain that a combination of corporatization and privatization automatically leads to depoliticization of firms. The reason is that politicians would attempt to influence even privatized firms by effectively buying allegiance with subsidies. Indeed, in Russia, initial stages of corporatization and privatization have been accompanied by an increase in subsidies to firms, as politicians strove to maintain output and employment in their favorite sectors despite the absence of demand for their products. Collective agriculture and defense, the two sectors that on efficiency grounds were the best candidates for shrinkage, have received the most money. To achieve depoliticization, the soft budget constraints of privatized firms have to harden, so that they maximize profits by succeeding in the marketplace rather than by catering to politicians in exchange for credits.[5] Although privatization by itself hardens the budget constraints of firms, meaningful post-privatization restructuring—the true benefit of an efficient ownership structure—requires further reforms, such as macroeconomic stabilization that curtails subsidies to privatized firms.

Moreover, when coalition building requires that cash flows in privatized firms go to shareholders other than the manager, such as the workers and the public, cash flows and control rights are no longer fully aligned. Since managers do not then fully pay for the consequences of their decisions, and since they may have objectives that do not serve shareholders, such as keeping their jobs, the resulting ownership structure is not fully efficient. This agency problem has been the focus of extensive analysis of publicly held corporations in market economies.[6] It is much more severe in Russia, where many managers are not fit for the job and need to be replaced.

The agency problem between managers and shareholders suggests that privatization is only the first step in getting cash flow and control rights aligned. The next step is ensuring effective corporate governance by transferring control rights from the managers to the outside shareholders who have the cash flow rights. Since outside shareholders are only interested in maximizing profits, the ownership structure that gives them both cash flow and control rights is truly efficient. Privatization is in fact typically accompanied by the creation of such corporate governance mechanisms that bring the ownership structure closer to efficiency.

Many writers on privatization in Eastern Europe and Russia have not viewed depoliticization as the primary goal of privatization, and have instead focused on establishing effective governance as the key objective.[7] In our view, controlling managers is not nearly as important as controlling politicians, since managers' interests are generally much closer to economic efficiency than those of the politicians. Once depoliticization is accomplished, the secondary goal of establishing effective corporate governance can be addressed. In chapter 5, we evaluate privatization from the perspective of corporate governance as well as depoliticization.

We conclude that a combination of corporatization and privatization offers the reformer the best opportunity to achieve efficient ownership. Politically this strategy may require a lot of coalition building, and, from the point of view of efficient ownership, it may be only the first step. Nonetheless, there is no strategy that is preferred from the efficiency viewpoint and is politically feasible. In the next chapter, then, we describe how this approach to achieving efficient ownership has been applied in Russia.

Notes

1. The situation becomes more complicated if the bureaucrat himself has an important investment in the project, or if contracts are not complete. See Sanford J. Grossman and Oliver D. Hart (1986), "The Costs and Benefits of Ownership: A Theory of Vertical and Lateral Integration," *Journal of Political Economy* 94, 691–719.

2. For a discussion of the efficiency effects of corruption, see Nathaniel Leff (1964), "Economic Development Through Bureaucratic Corruption," *American Behavioral Scientist,* 8–14; Samuel P. Huntington (1968), *Political Order in Changing Societies,* New Haven: Yale University Press; Andrei Shleifer and Robert W. Vishny (1993), "Corruption," *The Quarterly Journal of Economics* CVIII, 599–617, and (1994), "Politicians and Firms," *The Quarterly Journal of Economics* CIX, 995–1025.

3. For a recent socialist proposal along these lines see Pranab Bardhan and John E. Roemer (1992), "Market Socialism: A Case for Rejuvenation," *Journal of Economic Perspectives* 6, 101–116. For praise of East Asian bureaucracies, see Robert Wade (1990), *Governing the Market,* Princeton: University Press; and Alice H. Amsden (1989), *Asia's Next Giant,* New York: Oxford University Press.

4. On this, see Alwyn Young (1994), "The Tyranny of Numbers: Confronting the Statistical Realities of the East Asian Growth Experience," manuscript, Cambridge: Massachusetts Institute of Technology.

5. For an insightful discussion of soft budget constraints, see János Kornai (1992), *The Socialist System,* Princeton: University Press.

6. See Adolf A. Berle and Gardiner C. Means (1932), *The Modern Corporation and Private Property,* New York: Macmillan; and Michael C. Jensen and William H. Meckling (1976), "Theory of the Firm: Managerial Behavior, Agency Costs and the Ownership Structure," *Journal of Financial Economics* 3, 305–360.

7. Some of the studies that focus on corporate governance include David Lipton and Jeffrey D. Sachs (1990), "Privatization in Eastern Europe: The Case of Poland," *Brookings Papers on Economic Activity II*, 293–341; Edmund S. Phelps, Roman Frydman, Andrzej Rapaczynski, and Andrei Shleifer (1993), "Needed Mechanisms for Corporate Governance and Finance in Eastern Europe" in *The Economics of Transition* 1, No. 2; and Olivier J. Blanchard et al. (1991), *Reform in Eastern Europe,* Cambridge: MIT Press.

4

The Russian Privatization Program

We argued in chapter 3 that the most important objective of privatization is depoliticization of firms, or freeing them from politicians' control. The strategy for doing that is concentration of control and cash flow rights in the hands of enterprise managers and outside investors. We have also argued that, politically, privatization is very difficult to carry out. First, politicians as represented by sectoral ministries fiercely resist loss of control over business. Ultimately, they cannot be appeased, since the principal goal of privatization is precisely to disenfranchise those politicians. Second, other stakeholders in the firms, such as the workers and the local governments, have a claim to cash flow and control rights that must be addressed. The reformer cannot try to deprive these constituencies of their ownership claims and still hope to defeat the traditional politicians, unless he has absolute political power. Third, the principal ally of the reformer in his battle against political control has to be the public. Populist appeal is the most essential element of any privatization program that hopes to depoliticize the economy. In this chapter, we describe how the Russian privatizers, led by Chubais, designed a program that fought the politicians but gained other stakeholders as allies.

The political imperatives of privatization illuminate the first key controversy that developed over the design of the privatization program: should it take the form of cash sales or should it take the form of a free (or heavily subsidized) distribution of shares to insiders and the public, otherwise known as mass privatization? Most countries in the world, including those in Western Europe (including East Germany), Latin America, Asia, and Africa have conducted privatization programs through cash sales of assets. In cash sales, companies are either sold as a whole to the highest bidder, or else shares are placed in the market through a public offering. Firms privatized in cash sales generally separate from the government and increase their profits, productivity, and in some cases even employment.[1] Indeed, the assorted investment bankers giving advice in Russia, as well as many Gorbachev economists, advocated case-by-case privatization through cash sales.

To an economist, the efficiency case for privatization through sales is quite compelling. Sales take companies out of public hands and transfer them to private owners—the first step toward depoliticization. Sales also allocate companies to the most efficient owners, who are not necessarily the current managers, and thus speed up badly needed management turnover. To the extent that outside investors participate in these sales, they also can set up a proper governance and capital structure for the companies they buy, thereby addressing the problem of divergence of manager and shareholder interests immediately. Last but not least, privatization through sales generates revenue for the government, which is desperately needed in times of large budget deficits.

In light of these arguments, the fact that all East European governments have eschewed privatization through sales and opted for giveaways seems puzzling. For example, Jacques

Rogozinski, the head of the Mexican privatization program which applied the case-by-case method extremely successfully in the 1980s, entitled his 1993 highly critical article on Russia's mass privatization "Too Much Vodka!"[2] Nonetheless, upon closer scrutiny, the case for privatization through cash sales falls apart on both efficiency and especially political grounds.

From the point of view of efficiency, privatization through cash sales is just too slow. It requires valuation, information collection, preparation of auctions and public offerings and a variety of other services which investment banks gladly supply given ample time and generous fees. It is important to remember in this regard that West European countries typically privatize a few firms a year, and even such rapid privatizers as Mexico and Chile could handle at best a couple of hundred of firms per year. In contrast, Russia needed to privatize 25,000 medium- and large-scale firms. If these firms were properly valued, prepared for auctions, or, as some investment bankers wanted, restructured prior to sale, odds are privatization would have never gotten off the ground. Even if it did, at the rate of 200 per year, Russian privatization would have taken over a century! In the meantime, the economy would continue to stagnate.

From the political viewpoint, privatization through sales is even more problematic. To be politically feasible in Russia, this approach would have required the allocation of significant stakes to insiders at large discounts and only the remaining shares could be sold. Even such sales would probably have been resented, and certainly not supported, by the public at large. First, the highest bidders in cash privatizations often turn out to be illegitimate businessmen, former party and state security officials, and foreigners. Selling off the national patrimony to these investors generates public outrage rather than support.

Poland attempted a few privatizations through sales, but quickly ended the program once it became evident that the population saw it as a sellout to the Germans. Even the sales of East German companies to West German businessmen were extremely unpopular, notwithstanding the accompanying massive transfers of capital and know-how to the East. Second, privatization through sales offers no tangible benefit to the public at large, and hence cannot count on the essential public support in the battle against entrenched politicians. The way to make the public an ally in privatization is to distribute free shares to all citizens. Russia's reformers realized from the start that such mass privatization was the only politically viable way to achieve depoliticization.

The principal question, then, was how to design a mass privatization program. This chapter discusses the main elements of the Russian privatization program, but does not present its full legal content.[3] In brief, the privatization law was passed on July 3, 1991, before Yeltsin formed the Gaidar government. It looked very different from the eventual program, but shared with it the basic emphasis on giveaways. The Chubais privatization program was adopted by the government and the Parliament in June of 1992 after intense negotiations, and contained all the basic elements of corporatization and insider benefits, although not vouchers. Vouchers were chosen by Chubais as the mechanism of mass privatization in late spring 1992 and adopted by presidential decree in the summer.

We divide our discussion of the Russian program into four parts, which roughly correspond to the four essential elements of the program. In section 1, we focus on corporatization, and discuss its role in transferring control rights from the ministries to the managers, as well as in assuring that Russian companies became open stockholder societies rather than closed partnerships. In section 2, we describe the insider benefits eventually adopted in the Russian program, which were the subject of the principal political battles. In section 3, we discuss in broad terms the choice of vouchers as the vehicle of mass privatization in Russia. Once they were introduced, vouchers dominated both the politics and the economics of the Russian privatization; we try to explain why. In section 4, we outline some mechanical elements of voucher design and voucher auctions. In reform, details matter and the details of the Russian voucher privatization are likely to affect the evolution of ownership in Russia for some time. In section 5, we evaluate the Russian mass privatization strategy.

1 Corporatization

The Russian privatization program divided firms into those that would be sold as proprietorships for cash, usually by the local governments, and those that would go into the mass privatization program. In this way, most shops and some smaller firms were immediately allocated to the local governments, which demanded the revenues from small-scale privatization as their major concession (although later on small shops were sold for vouchers as well). We do not deal with small-scale privatization in this book, except to note that it was important in bringing local governments into a coalition supporting mass privatization.[4]

The program then divided the larger firms into those subject to mandatory privatization, those subject to privatization with the permission of GKI, those requiring cabinet approval for privatization, and those whose privatization was prohibited. Mandatory privatization included firms in the light industries such as textiles, food processing, and furniture. Firms requiring

GKI approval tended to be the larger manufacturing firms, but not the ones operating in the key strategic industries. Major firms in most strategic industries, such as natural resources and defense, could only be privatized with the approval of the whole cabinet. Given the anti-reformist composition of the cabinet in 1993, this restriction meant that many of these firms were not privatized. Even if some part of their equity could be privately owned, control always remained with politicians. Finally, firms in sectors such as railroad transport, space exploration, health, and education could not be privatized at all.

A Western reader of the privatization program in 1992 would quickly note these restrictions taking roughly a third of the text, and wonder: How could a real privatization program spend so much time stressing what cannot be privatized? In fact, this catalogue of exceptions proved critical in restricting the scope of ministerial as well as GKI interference in privatization of individual firms. The ministries lost their principal battle for control when they lost the right to approve the privatization plans of the majority of firms in exchange for power over privatization of strategic firms. The task of wresting control over strategic firms from the ministries was left to their managers.

All firms above a certain level of employment and assets, except for those on the prohibited list, were to be corporatized. That is to say, they were to re-register as joint stock companies with 100 percent of equity owned by the government, a corporate charter, and a board of directors. Initially, the board would have representation by the government, the firm's general manager (with two votes), the workers, and the local government. Boards of directors did not have any representation by outside investors. The corporatization decree, signed by President Yeltsin in June of 1992, was the first major step toward subsequent privatization of state firms.

To corporatize a company, the management had to value it in order to determine charter capital. The idea of revaluing Russian companies using proper accounting methods and adjusting for inflation appealed to many Westerners, as well as to the Russian bureaucrats who saw an opportunity to adjust valuations in exchange for bribes. One of the hardest-fought battles of privatization was to resist these attempts at valuation, and to simply declare that the book value of Russian companies as of July 1992, without any adjustment, would serve as the charter capital. This avoidance of bureaucratic interference proved critical, largely because it took away from Moscow ministries a key control right. The privatization program did not ultimately rely on valuations.

Corporatization significantly undermined the power of central ministries. Corporatized firms were governed by their boards of directors rather than by industrial ministries. Moreover, the government's member of the board of directors was to come not from the ministry under which the firm fell but from the government shareholding agency (the State Property Fund). As a result, ministries lost their remaining legal control rights over firms in corporatization.

By insisting that firms convert to open joint stock companies, corporatization also prevented the conversion of the vast majority of Russian firms into closed companies owned by their workers and managers, following the pattern of collective farms. The problems of such companies are well known: they cannot raise capital, they do not easily accommodate conflicts between the owners, and their managers cannot be removed through external governance mechanisms. These problems also make closed companies very difficult to depoliticize, since their isolation from external markets reinforces their dependence on, and vulnerability to, political control through the state's supply of capital. Because many Russian managers preferred to assure their complete control through forming closed rather than open companies, they opposed the corporatization decree. To convince managers and workers to form an open company, they had to be given many additional enticements.

Parallel to corporatization, divisions of state firms had the right to split off and become independent. This proved to be rather difficult because of resistance from the management of the holding company and local officials. Nonetheless, such split-offs occurred in many cases, and facilitated a spontaneous restructuring of some giant Russian conglomerates in a situation where restructuring by politicians was not workable.

2 Insider Benefits

The claim of employees on the shares of their firms was recognized in Russia from the start. Even the July 1991 privatization law offered many benefits to the employees. In the spring of 1992, the notion of providing large benefits for workers in privatization received enormous political support. The idea of the means of production belonging to the workers had a great deal of historical appeal in Russia, and carried substantial support from the workers' lobby as well as among voters generally. Many enterprise managers also favored the idea of turning firms over to their managers and workers for free, especially if firms could then be transformed into closed partnerships. Managers felt that they could control the workers' collectives and feared outside interference much more than that of their own employees. In the end, they proved to be right.

Despite the fact that managers stood to gain a lot from privatization, they were in a position to bargain for even more. In the last years of socialism, the communist managers found themselves in a comfortable position: they had sharply increased control over their firms and they still were receiving subsidies. The managers recognized that privatization would make them richer, but it would also require more work and potentially create an external threat to their control. Moreover, many managers, particularly of defense firms that found themselves starved of orders when Russia began demilitarizing, recognized that privatization threatened them with bankruptcy. These managers controlled a powerful lobby in the Parliament, Arkady Volsky's Civic Union. It was clear from the start that the Russian managers, even more so than the workers, would have to receive generous inducements to support privatization.

Because the managers and the workers had a common interest, giving enterprises completely to them was probably the single most commonly discussed alternative to the government's privatization program in the spring of 1992. It was supported by various Russian politicians, of whom the most vocal was Larisa Pyasheva, the head of Moscow City privatization who proudly wore a pin from the libertarian Cato Institute on her lapel. Despite her impressive capitalist rhetoric, Ms. Pyasheva simply turned Moscow shops over to their workers, which was far from the best strategy from the viewpoint of restructuring. Complete insider control was also supported by a significant part of the managerial and worker lobbies, since it meant exclusion of outsiders. Finally, it was loudly supported by various worker ownership zealots from the United States, who, spurned in their native country, sought easy glory in Russia. The Gorbachev Foundation, the retirement home of the last Soviet leader, became the intellectual home of many of these ideas.

The trouble with running large industrial firms as partnerships of managers and workers is that this organizational form usually does not work. Raising capital and resolving disputes between shareholders become insurmountable problems, and as a result these firms have to ask politicians for help. For this reason, privatization officials, while recognizing the need to be generous to managers and workers, strenuously resisted this proposal. Instead, the privatization program offered managers and workers a package of benefits that came to be called Option 1. It offered workers 25 percent of the shares in their firm for free, but made these shares nonvoting to prevent worker control. Workers could buy an additional 10 percent of the shares at a 30 percent discount from book value, which was set at a very low level, as well as some extra shares for the pension plan. Top managers received 5 percent of the shares at a nominal price. These benefits to the workers and managers far exceeded those offered in any other privatization ever attempted in the world.

Despite its generosity, Option 1 proved to be insufficient, since worker and manager interest groups held sway in Parliament. The compromise between Chubais and Parliament was Option 2, the employee-management buy out, which allowed managers and workers together to buy 51 percent of the voting equity at a nominal price of 1.7 times the July 1992 book value of assets. The multiple of 1.7 was said to be based on calculations made by GKI experts, and looked scientific enough to deter critics who demanded individualized revaluations of all Russian companies. The approach worked, and 1.7 was accepted as a reasonable multiple, making assets available to workers at extremely low prices in light of the prevailing inflation rate. Under Option 2, workers could pay for their shares in cash, with vouchers, or with the retained earnings of the firm, and could extend payments over some relatively short period of time. As with the first option, some additional shares could be bought for the pension plan. In short, the Parliament offered insiders control over privatized firms.

Although Chubais fought Option 2, he was bound to fail given the sentiment in Parliament. Instead, he accepted Option 2 but insisted to the end that workers own their shares as individuals rather than as collectives, and be free to sell their shares any time they want. The freedom to sell shares did much to encourage corporate governance in Russia, and saved it from the dominance of closed partnerships in industry. Equally important, Option 2 effectively bought the political support of enough legislators representing worker and manager interests that the privatization program could be passed.

On a suggestion of a people's deputy from Irkutsk, the Parliament also introduced a third option of manager and worker benefits, which allowed the managers to buy up to 40 percent of the shares at very low prices if they promised not to go bankrupt. Luckily, this option did not go very far. First, a compromise with Chubais restricted the applicability of this option to small firms, since he argued that turning thousands of managers into multi-millionaires overnight would incite popular outrage. Second, since the bankruptcy procedure was not yet defined, every Russian manager feared (not without reason) being declared bankrupt by a bribe-seeking bureaucrat and losing control, which reduced the appeal of Option 3. Third, the regulations on Option 3 were written in traditional Russian bureaucratese, which meant that hardly anyone, including the managers, could understand them. Chubais's advisors did not volunteer to clarify the language of these regulations. For these three reasons, hardly any companies chose Option 3.

Along with corporatization of a firm, its workers' collective, guided by its managers, had the right under the privatization program to select its benefits option. Choice in selecting the benefits option proved popular, as managers and workers' collectives felt that they could shape their future. Taking the workers' selection into account, the managers then had to submit to their local GKI office a privatization plan that described how the rest of the shares were to be sold. The principal forms of sale were voucher auctions and investment tenders, which we describe below. While some firms were subject to mandatory privatization, in practice the filing of privatization plans was almost always voluntary. This is probably the single most important benefit that the managers received in the privatization program: within certain guidelines, they, rather than any ministerial or other government officials, had almost complete control over the strategy for privatizing their firms. While privatization plans of strategic firms had to be approved in Moscow, for most firms they could be approved locally, where managers could usually agree with officials. The local officials were also happy that they, rather than outsiders, approved privatization plans. By pushing the privatization process onto firms, Chubais deprived the ministries and other Moscow politicians of their most important tool of control, the right to withhold signatures. More than anything else, this bottom-up approach depoliticized the privatization process itself.

Although Option 2 allowed the adoption of the privatization program by Parliament, the debate over alternative privatization strategies did not end. The politicians who favored worker ownership continued to criticize the program and push their own ideas. More importantly, officials in the ministries began to recognize that privatization clearly spelled their end since it robbed them of their control rights and handed those rights over to the managers. In the spring and summer of 1992, the sectoral ministries started advocating the idea of a new privatization mechanism through the creation of financial-industrial groups, which would be very large clusters of enterprises linked by supply chains and coordinated by the ministries. One proposal along these lines, pushed by the Minister of Industry Alexander Titkin, gained some support in the cabinet. Catering to the insiders thus did not buy the privatization program full security. To gain security, it had to appeal to the public. For that, it needed vouchers.

3 The Choice of Voucher Privatization

The fragility of the political coalition supporting privatization made it imperative for reformers to seek public support for their program. The support of the professionals, the students, the retirees, the military personnel and others was needed to quash the notion that only enterprise workers and managers should enjoy the benefits of privatization. But even with this notion defeated, it was quite clear that, once managers and workers got their benefits, they could easily insist on getting more out of the unsold shares. To be sustainable, the privatization program had to pit the interests of the public at large against those of the workers and the managers.

Some of the general principles of how to do this were clear from the start. Shares in privatizing firms had to be distributed to the public free or at a nominal charge. The procedure for doing this had to be simple and transparent to avoid the impression that the government was using mass privatization to enrich its friends. Such skepticism was only natural in Russia given its past experience with communist politicians, and ironically was voiced by the communists themselves. Finally, to make the program sustainable, the public had to actively participate in the process rather than just passively receive some pieces of paper.

The experiences of Poland and the Czech Republic offered Russia two distinct approaches to mass privatization: mutual funds and vouchers. The Polish mass privatization program called for the creation of about twenty mutual funds managed by foreign investment banks, which would administratively receive shares in roughly 400 privatizing industrial firms. Each firm would have a lead fund with a controlling block of shares, as well as other funds as minority shareholders. Each Polish citizen would receive a tradeable share in each of these mutual funds. The program had the advantages of simplicity and transparency, but also endowed each privatizing firm with a large shareholder who could oversee its restructuring and encourage foreign investors. The Polish mass privatization scheme thus addressed the corporate governance issue head-on.

The alternative approach, tried most successfully in the Czech Republic, was to issue vouchers to the population at a nominal charge, and to sell shares in privatizing firms in exchange for these vouchers. This approach also had the advantage of being relatively simple and transparent, although it was more complicated than the Polish scheme, since it relied on auctions rather than direct share distribution. More importantly, the evidence coming from the Czech Republic showed that the Czech public was much more interested in privatization than was the public in Poland, since people had the choice of how to use their vouchers. The voucher scheme in the Czech Republic paid much less attention to creating core investors. Private mutual funds were encouraged, and in fact dozens were formed and became very large investors in the Czech companies. Nonetheless, these funds were not created by government design and firms were not guaranteed effective corporate governance.

For reasons of both efficiency and politics, Russia opted for a voucher scheme in many ways similar to that used by the Czechs rather than the Polish model. From the efficiency viewpoint, it was (and still is) by no means clear that foreign-run mutual funds in Poland could successfully achieve depoliticization. It was hard to imagine some 35-year-old British or American investment banker telling a Polish manager to sack 3,000 people, without this manager calling some minister or legislator and demanding that the foreigner be ignored. The Polish funds were designed to be too large and too political to be real engines of depoliticization. Foreign control of these funds only raised the likelihood that firms would become vulnerable to political influence. This problem was obviously going to be at least as severe in Russia as in Poland. In fact, we believed in 1992 that the emphasis on corporate governance rather than depoliticization was the fundamental conceptual error of the Polish approach to privatization.

From the political viewpoint, the signals coming from Poland and Czechoslovakia in 1992 made it clear that the Czechs were excited about privatization and involved in it, while the Poles were not. Choice made all the difference. Since popular involvement was deemed absolutely essential for the sustainability of Russian privatization, vouchers were a clear choice.

The privatization program offered all citizens including children, for a nominal payment of 25 rubles, an opportunity to receive a voucher with a denomination of 10,000 rubles. Each citizen could sell his voucher in an open market without any restrictions, turn it over to a private voucher investment fund to invest for him, or use it personally to buy shares in his own company or at a voucher auction of any privatizing company in the country. The right to sell vouchers proved critical in creating a number of active external shareholders in Russia, who accumulated blocks of vouchers and used them to buy shares. The private mutual funds also played a key role as investors in Russian stocks. Through vouchers, reformers managed to promote significant outside investment in shares of privatizing firms, a feat that would have been difficult to accomplish in any other way.

Privatizing firms typically sold 29 percent of their shares at auction, although the so-called strategic enterprises sold less and more was retained in government hands. Voucher auctions were conducted individually and locally, which gave local officials some ability to discourage unwanted investors. The largest firms were sold through national voucher auctions, which enabled people throughout the country to buy their shares without having to travel.

Vouchers were announced by President Yeltsin in August 1992 and distributed between October and February. They quickly became the defining feature of Russian privatization, and probably of the whole economic reform effort. Most importantly, they did what they were supposed to do, namely to assure that there would be no turning back on privatization. Vouchers represented real value given by the government to the public; cancelling the program would have constituted confiscation of people's assets. The government became a hostage of vouchers, and hence, despite all its divisions and frequent anti-reformist sentiments, could only reverse the reform at a prohibitive political cost. The parliamentary hardliners said that vouchers were a good idea in principle, though they wanted them to be used not for the "worthless" shares of privatizing firms, but for expenditures useful to the people, such as education and healthcare. They proposed issuing vouchers for these purposes as well, especially since they were as cheap to print as money. When Chernomyrdin became Prime Minister in December 1992, he compared privatization to Stalin's bloody collectivization of agriculture in a venomous speech to St. Petersburg industrial managers. Yeltsin harshly criticized him, and shortly afterward Chernomyrdin dropped his opposition. With vouchers in the hands of 144 million Russian citizens, the prime minister made a prudent decision.

4 Vouchers and Voucher Auctions

Adopting vouchers as the privatization vehicle was the most important political and economic decision of the Russian privatization. But going from there to selling off thousands of firms was also a matter of designing a program that addressed the economic and political objectives of the reformers. In this section, we briefly describe the details of voucher privatization in Russia, and compare it to that in the Czech Republic to highlight some differences. We focus on two areas: how the voucher itself was designed as the privatization vehicle and how voucher auctions were conducted. In both of these areas, the Czech Republic and Russia adopted very different approaches, largely because of the different politics of the two countries.

The Russian Voucher

Although a voucher is just a piece of paper exchangeable for shares in privatizing companies, its design raised several critical questions. Should vouchers be denominated in cash or in points? Russia opted for the former strategy, while the Czech Republic chose the latter. Should vouchers be tradeable? Unlike most countries, including Lithuania, Mongolia, and the Czech Republic, Russia allowed free trading in vouchers. What were the reasons for these choices in voucher design?

There are many good reasons for denominating vouchers in points. First, such vouchers clearly are not currency, which makes them less money-like. If people use vouchers as money for purchases, the effective money supply and the price level rise. Second, denominating vouchers in points avoids the risk that vouchers trade at a discount to face value, making people feel cheated. In Russia, vouchers were issued with the face value of 10,000 rubles, but within the first two months fell to a discount of 60 percent in market trading, creating a serious political problem. Denominating vouchers in points as the Czechs did definitely eliminates this problem.

At the same time, denominating vouchers in currency has one important political advantage, which was why Chubais adopted this strategy. Specifically, a currency denomination makes vouchers appear like securities and gives a clearer impression of a government gift to the public. In Russia, where initial public acceptance of privatization was much more tenuous than in the Czech Republic, the popularity of a free gift from the government was badly needed. Moreover, denomination in currency made a much stronger commitment to irreversibility. It is one thing to cancel privatization after people received booklets with points; it is quite another to cancel privatization after they have been given securities with a face value of 10,000 rubles. For these reasons, Chubais accepted the possibility of unpopular discounts and chose to give vouchers a currency denomination.

Perhaps the greatest innovation of Russian privatization was the free tradeability of vouchers. The main argument against free tradeability is that vouchers are not currency or securities, but rather vehicles for implementing privatization. Unless converted into shares, they should not be treated as securities. The second argument against free tradeability, a paternalistic one, is that when the market value of vouchers is lower than the true value of underlying assets, letting vouchers trade enables rich buyers to take advantage of poor sellers. Finally, allowing vouchers to trade may cause "speculative excesses." These arguments carried the day in most countries. The Czech Republic, Lithuania, Mongolia and others all prohibited the trading of vouchers.

In a rare display of liberalism, Russia permitted free trading. The reasons were both political and economic. Tradeability lets people convert vouchers to cash right away, which especially helps the poor who have great immediate consumption needs. These people would view privatization as a usable, if small, giveaway and presumably support it. Tradeability is thus consistent with both the importance of choice in voucher privatization, including the choice not to become an owner, and with the protection of the poor. Moreover, trading in vouchers would take place even if it were forbidden, as it did in Mongolia, with the result that the poor receive low prices in illiquid markets. The best price protection is to permit competitive and open markets for vouchers. If people can check the price several places, and if voucher buyers compete, prices should be reasonably fair.

The second reason for allowing free trade in vouchers is that it vastly improves opportunities for potential large investors. To acquire large blocks of shares in voucher auctions, potential investors would have to assemble large quantities of vouchers. This would be extremely expensive without organized voucher markets. Such markets thus not only offer a better deal to individual voucher holders, but also improve opportunities for block accumulation and thereby foster better corporate governance. As a side benefit, the daily price of a voucher presented the reformers with a reliable barometer of the market's perception of the likely success of reforms.

Voucher Auctions

In designing voucher privatization, the critical issue is how to exchange vouchers for shares in companies. The obvious strategy is to run auctions of company shares. Auctions have tremendous economic and political benefits. First, they generally allocate shares to those who value them most, and hence are more efficient than other allocation mechanisms. Second, auctions produce market valuations of companies from the start and hence facilitate subsequent trading. Third, auctions do not require bureaucrats to value companies, which avoids arbitrariness, delays, and corruption. Fourth, auctions are much less susceptible to sales to cronies at low prices than direct sales. Fifth, auctions give people choice of what shares, if any, to buy—thereby fulfilling one of the political imperatives of mass privatization. For both economic and political reasons, then, all countries using vouchers have opted for auctions over fixed-price and discretionary sales.

Designing auctions for mass privatization imposes a host of requirements that do not often arise in the discussions of regular auctions. First, these auctions must be administratively simple so that bureaucrats can actually run them. Second, it must be possible for millions of investors to bid even when they know next to nothing about either auctions or the companies up for sale. Third, these investors, as a rule, must succeed in getting shares in auctions. They cannot feel shut out by being routinely outbid by professionals, which would undermine the populist appeal of mass privatization. Fourth, the auction procedure should assure that small investors do not end up paying more for shares than professionals do. These four criteria all have to do with administrative feasibility and political attractiveness of auctions.

These criteria raise many questions of auction design. Should auctions be centralized, with shares of each company sold *simultaneously*, or should the privatization authorities auction shares of one firm at a time? How can auctions be kept relatively simple for investors and auction administrators? How can bid-rigging be avoided? Below we describe some answers.

Centralization of Auctions   The Czech Republic and Russia have followed different strategies on how to auction shares. In the Czech scheme, auctions took the form of centralized price adjustment mechanisms over several rounds. First, shares of all companies were put on the market simultaneously at fixed prices that were loosely related to values. Voucher holders then presented their quantity demands at these prices for the shares they wanted. If the total demand for shares of some company at the initial price fell below the number of shares available, then the demands were satisfied at that price, and the price was reduced for the next round. If the demand exceeded supply by only a small margin, bidders got proportionately fewer shares than they asked for and the bidding for the stock ended. If the demand exceeded supply by a greater amount, nobody got any shares and the price of the stock was increased for the next round. The rules for price changes were not publicly disclosed.

This procedure had several advantages. First, although it took several months to complete, when it was finished all the shares were actually allocated and firms were privatized. Second, the centralized approach left no room for external interference from managers that could delay auctions of individual companies. As a result, managers could not as easily avoid privatization as they could with a decentralized procedure. Third, the centralized procedure had the main efficiency benefits of auctions, namely that bidders who valued a stock the most got it in the end, and that some initial market price was established.

Russia had vastly more companies and more auction participants than the Czech Republic, so the centralized procedure seemed unmanageable. More importantly, because it was politically much more credible, the Czech government could pull almost all companies into privatization without the consent of the managers. In Russia, in contrast, privatization had to start on a voluntary basis, with managers of companies who wanted to privatize leading the way. Moreover, managers had to have some control over when their company was privatized and what fraction of shares was offered for vouchers. In addition, local officials demanded control over voucher auctions, particularly of companies of regional importance. To get the consent of the managers and the local officials, voucher auctions had to be decentralized and pushed to localities. Once this was done, managers of many companies realized that they could profit from privatization and did not need to fear the immediate takeover of their company. As a result, many more consented to putting their company through the program, and even pushed local (and Moscow) officials to accommodate them. Privatization took off. A more centralized procedure could have encountered strong enough opposition from some managers and local officials to subvert privatization.

Designing a Simple Voucher Auction A theoretically correct voucher auction would call for each bidder to submit the number of shares he wants and the maximum price he is willing to pay. To millions of participants, who have no knowledge of the real value of privatizing companies, such an auction might seem impossibly difficult. For example, such auctions might lead to situations in which small investors get no shares of desirable companies because they anchor their bids to book values, while true values are much higher, and get all the shares of the bad companies which professional investors avoid. This outcome would create a political backlash against privatization. The theoretically correct auction, then, does not meet the requirement of bid simplicity and accessibility to small investors.

To save small investors from the need to make complicated bids, one strategy is to ask each investor to submit his voucher as a bid for the company. The equilibrium number of shares each voucher buys is then inversely proportional to the number of vouchers tendered. Thus, if the company offers 1,000 shares for auction, and 40 vouchers are submitted, then each voucher buys 25 shares. If, on the other hand, 4,000 vouchers are submitted, each voucher buys only a quarter of a share. Each investor submitting vouchers is assured of getting some shares, but gets fewer shares of desirable companies.

This simple auction design has several advantages. First, the bids are extremely simple: investors just need to tender their vouchers. Second, small investors *always* receive some shares for their vouchers. They are never turned down. Third, all investors pay the same price in the auction and large investors do not get any advantages. From the perspective of administrative simplicity and attractiveness to small investors, this auction looks hard to beat.

The problem with this auction is that sophisticated investors, who might have information about share values and who therefore could bring about accurate company valuation in an auction, could influence the price only by changing the number of vouchers they tender. In general, they would like more room to maneuver. To address this problem, voucher auctions allowed, in addition to simple bids, the so-called type 2 bids, in which an investor could specify the maximum price (in vouchers per share) he was willing to pay. To arrive at the equilibrium price, simple and type 2 bids were just added up. This procedure was used in virtually every single Russian auction, with no complaints about manipulation or other problems. Interestingly, type 2 bids were used by fewer than 2 percent of the bidders, and typically not by large sophisticated investors, who simply brought suitcases full of vouchers to the auctions and turned them in. The reason is that, if a type 2 bidder did not get shares in a voucher auction, it often took local officials three to four months to return his vouchers, during which he could not use them elsewhere. It was easier to make a type 1 bid and get shares for sure than to deal with auction administrators for the next three months. Even this mild attempt by the designers of voucher auctions to promote efficient pricing fell victim to the overwhelming need for simple procedures in which officials played little or no role.

We have discussed voucher auctions in so much detail for a simple reason. Although economists know how to construct very sophisticated auctions, when auctions were used in Russian privatization, political considerations determined their design. Auctions had to be simplified and adjusted to political reality, although most of their major economic benefits were preserved. Despite the shortcuts that had to be made, voucher auctions worked well, and have facilitated the transfer of vast amounts of property to private owners.

5 An Assessment

To secure political support, Russia's privatizers had to make compromises and give in to the demands of major interest groups. Local governments, managers, and workers all got much more out of privatization than most observers would consider reasonable.

Local governments won control over, and most revenues from, small-scale privatization. They would have received revenues from large-scale privatization as well, except that the means of payment was vouchers. Moreover, because voucher auctions were run locally, local governments had some limited opportunity to exclude undesirable outsiders from participating. Thanks to these concessions, local governments, with a few exceptions in war-torn regions, nationalist enclaves, the Far East, and the city of Moscow, did not resist privatization.

With Option 2, workers received the most generous concessions of any privatization in the world. It is important to remember, however, that at the time the program was proposed, the demand for 100 percent worker ownership presented the greatest threat to privatization. Only by offering high worker ownership did the reformers succeed in defeating the ministries and their allies.

Concessions to the managers were even larger. Although the initial ownership stakes of managers were limited in both Option 1 and Option 2, in many cases managers bought more cheap shares in voucher auctions or in the aftermarket from employees. An even more important concession to the managers was that the privatization program did not impose large shareholders on the firm, so managerial independence in Russia, at least ex ante, was much greater than elsewhere in Eastern Europe. Insistence on core investors would have raised strong managerial opposition and made privatization impossible, especially since privatization in Russia was effectively discretionary.

On top of all this, the Russian privatizers allocated 29 percent of all firms to the public, just to win their active support.

This political accommodation showed how wrong it would have been to think of the government as the sole owner of the assets. The stakeholders in Russian industry had many ownership rights as well, and large concessions were needed to co-opt them. But the payoff was worth it, since the three main benefits of privatization from the efficiency standpoint were preserved.

First, although concessions were spread rather wide, the ministries received hardly any. They were given no role on boards of directors, in the preparation or approval of privatization plans (except in a few strategic companies), or in voucher auctions. Their great ideas about financial-industrial groups directed by former ministries never came to pass. With the help of the stakeholders, reformers broke the backs of the Russian ministries. Since the program's main objective was depoliticization, this was a vital accomplishment.

Second, the privatization program avoided the conversion of industrial companies into collective-farm-style partnerships, which was a real and serious danger. Because shares were always tradeable, and were held by workers as individuals, the possibility of reallocation of shares from the workers to other investors was built in from the start. This too proved to be important.

Finally, individuals were allowed to sell their vouchers or give them to voucher funds (these options were in fact listed on the back of each voucher). The trading of vouchers, and the concentration of vouchers in investment funds, have stimulated both the creation of outside shareholders and even the concentration of shareholdings in Russian companies by both managers and outside directors. This too had significant implications for efficient ownership.

Over time, all three of these elements of the program would become critical in promoting the restructuring of Russian industry and thus enhancing its performance.

Notes

1. Recent studies of post-privatization restructuring include William L. Megginson, Robert C. Nash and Mathias van Randenborgh (1994), "The Financial and Operating Performance of Newly Privatized Firms: An International Empirical Analysis," *Journal of Finance*, XLIX, 403–452; Florencio Lopez-de-Silanes (1993), "Determinants of Privatization Prices," manuscript, Harvard University; and Nicholas Barberis, Maxim Boycko, Andrei Shleifer and Natalia Tsukanova (1994), "How Does Privatization Work? Evidence from the Russian Shops," manuscript, Harvard University.

2. Jacques Rogozinski (1993), "Too Much Vodka!" *The International Economy*, 52–54.

3. A detailed presentation of the Russian program is contained in Roman Frydman, Andrzej Rapaczynski, John S. Earle, et al. (1993), *The Privatization Process in Central Europe*, London: Central European University Press.

4. The rules of small-scale privatization in Russia are described in John Earle, Roman Frydman, Andrzej Rapaczynski, and Joel Turkewitz (1994), *Small Privatization*, Budapest: Central European University Press.

5

Results of Russian Privatization

Between October 1992 and June 1994, the privatization program described in the previous chapter was implemented by GKI. In this chapter, we describe what actually happened. In sections 1 through 3, we present a detailed account of corporatization, voucher use, and voucher auctions. All the principal elements of the Russian privatization program worked largely as planned, and the program turned into a rare success story of Russian economic reform.

In the second part of this chapter, we turn to an assessment of Russian privatization from the theoretical perspective of chapter 2. Our analysis is limited in part by the fact that Russian privatization is very recent, and in part by a lack of quality data.

In section 4, we look at how the shareholders in privatized firms exercise corporate control. We examine whether the interest of outside investors, which is probably the closest to profit maximization, is actually being served. Section 4 concludes that privatization has moved Russian firms only part of the way toward efficient ownership.

In section 5, we examine the market values of privatized companies. Relative to Western benchmarks, market values of privatized Russian companies implied by prices in voucher auctions were extremely low. Consistent with section 4, the valuation evidence suggests that, at the time of voucher auctions, firms were not expected to cater to outside investors, and many still do not. Political influence on firms and managerial self-dealing have not disappeared.

In section 6, we evaluate the significance of the changes to date. The Russian economy has made a giant step toward efficient ownership. Firms were depoliticized to a greater extent than anyone had expected, and the foundations of a viable market for corporate control have been put in place. However, much remains to be done to bring companies closer to efficient ownership.

1 Corporatization

By the end of voucher privatization, GKI and its regional offices registered over 22,000 firms as joint-stock companies. An average corporatized firm had over 1,000 employees. The apparent enthusiasm for corporatization confirms the generosity of worker and manager benefits. The managers dominated the meetings of the workers' collectives in most firms, and made proposals that the workers rubber-stamped. In 73 percent of firms, workers and managers selected Option 2, which gave them voting control. In 25 percent of firms, they chose Option 1. In most cases, the stated reason for choosing Option 2 was the fear that otherwise control might fall to outsiders. Option 1 was chosen when the company was too capital intensive for workers and their families to afford Option 2, as in the case of energy companies, or when the relationship between workers and managers was sufficiently tense that the managers feared giving workers voting shares. Option 3 was hardly ever chosen.

Following the selection of the benefits option, firms submitted their privatization plans to local offices of GKI. Many firms attempted to deviate from the standard formula of offering 29 percent of shares for vouchers, and tried to allocate shares to suppliers and customers, as well as more to insiders. Most managers disliked open and competitive voucher auctions. But because of GKI's insistence and Yeltsin's decree in August 1993, most firms eventually adhered to the standard formula, sometimes by running a second voucher auction to get up to 29 percent.

In addition, most firms proposed in their privatization plans to hold investment tenders, in which the stake that the government kept after a voucher auction, about 20 percent, would be sold to a core investor in exchange for a commitment to future investment in the company. Some of the better companies planned to use the investment tender to attract foreign capital; others hoped to use it to get more shares for insiders who would borrow money to buy out the government's stake. Investment tenders became popular because managers generally controlled them much more tightly than either voucher auctions or cash sales. Local GKIs generally approved privatization plans quickly, although strategic enterprises, which required signatures from sectoral ministries and central GKI, had to wait longer. In early 1994, under tremendous pressure from the managers who wanted to privatize, these approvals came as well.

2 Voucher Distribution and Use

Between October 1992 and January 1993, all 147 million Russians were given an opportunity to pick up their vouchers at the local branches of the State Savings Bank. The fee for obtaining each voucher was only 25 rubles (10 cents at the prevailing exchange rate). Because privatization in Russia was designed to be much more populist than privatization in the Czech Republic, the idea of charging a reasonable participation fee ($35 in the Czech Republic) to eliminate marginally interested citizens was rejected. By the end of January 1993, 144 million vouchers, or almost 98 percent of the total, had been picked up.

Shortly after its introduction, the voucher became the first liquid security in modern Russia, actively traded throughout the country. Young entrepreneurs went door to door buying vouchers from people willing to part with them. Street kiosks across the land turned into retail buying points as well. The entrepreneurs then sold vouchers in large blocks on dozens of regional exchanges to potential investors. On the largest exchange in Moscow, the Russian Commodity and Raw Materials Exchange, volume quickly reached 60–100 thousand vouchers per day, which added up to close to $1 million at prevailing prices. Toward the end of the auctions, the daily volume rose to $10 million. Apparently, investors in voucher auctions did not experience major problems in assembling large blocks of vouchers.

People used their vouchers in a variety of ways. Many sold them for cash. About 12 million people used vouchers in closed subscriptions for their own company shares. Another 10 million used them individually in voucher auctions. Most of those who invested their vouchers turned them over to privately created voucher investment funds, which began to spring up in the summer of 1993. Eventually, over 600 funds were formed. They collected 45 million vouchers from 23 million citizens. Although some of these funds were explicitly formed by industrial companies to buy up their own shares, most large funds operated as financial institutions. The largest fund in Moscow, First Voucher, used heavy television advertising to amass over 4 million vouchers. The voucher funds began their activity by speculating in vouchers on the exchanges but eventually became significant investors in privatizing firms. Though far from perfect, these funds turned out to be more reliable investment vehicles than the many Ponzi schemes offered to Russian investors at the time, such as the infamous MMM. Very few funds simply stole vouchers from investors. In the worst episode of this type, the management of NeftAlmazInvest, a fund promising to invest in the oil and diamond industries, got away with about 900,000 vouchers, although some of them were subsequently recovered. As consolidators of vouchers and shares, voucher funds became both key participants in privatization and critical players in the emerging securities market.

In the 20 months of the voucher program, the voucher price reached a low of $4 and a high above $20, with many swings in between thanks to the changing political winds (Figure 5.1). After a good start in late 1992, the fall of the Gaidar government in mid-December led to a collapse of the voucher price. From January through April, the large number of voucher auctions and closed subscriptions notwithstanding, the voucher price stagnated, hitting a low of a little over $4. The voucher price doubled in just a few weeks following Yeltsin's victory in the referendum on April 25, which revealed strong public support for economic reform. In the summer of 1993, the Parliament unleashed its most aggressive attack on privatization. Not surprisingly, the voucher price fell again. The voucher rose to new heights following Yeltsin's disbanding of

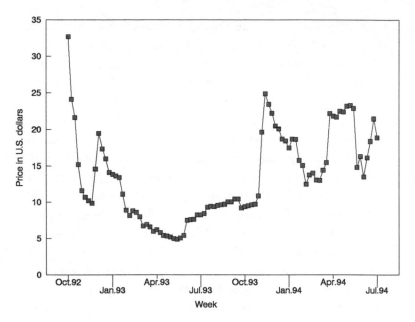

Figure 5.1.
Voucher prices in U.S. dollars.

the Parliament in September, but fell sharply after the poor
showing of reformers in the December 1993 elections. Once it
became clear that privatization would continue despite these
setbacks, the voucher price began to rise. In the last two
months of privatization, the voucher traded around $20, in
part because foreign investors entered the market and bought
large blocks of vouchers. The price of the few vouchers still
outstanding did not collapse when the voucher program ended
because Yeltsin decreed that vouchers would still be usable in
the fall. Despite the wide swings, even the highest voucher price
represented an extremely low valuation of Russian industry, a
fact we try to explain at the end of this chapter.

3 Voucher Auctions

The first company sold in a voucher auction by the official rules was the Bolshevik Cake Factory in Moscow. Although the auction was carefully planned to be a showcase for the program, there were a few last-minute hurdles. The investment bank Credit Suisse First Boston (CSFB), which was hired to run the auction, initially announced that GKI's procedure for selling shares for vouchers was unworkable. They later warmed up to it. Right before the auction, the director of Bolshevik announced that he was negotiating a subsidized loan with the government, and wanted to postpone the event until he was finished. He only agreed to proceed once assured that privatization would not endanger his loan. With these hurdles out of the way, CSFB rented a large hall and hired a couple hundred people to deal with what they feared would be tens of thousands of Moscovites lining up for Bolshevik shares. Fortunately, the European Bank for Reconstruction and Development footed the bill for the event. The Bolshevik auction proceeded smoothly, although only a few hundred friends and relatives of Bolshevik employees showed up to buy shares, as did representatives of one of Moscow's most aggressive voucher funds, Alpha Capital. Bolshevik received massive coverage in the press, and CSFB went on to become the premier Western broker in Russia. Privatization was off to a good start.

In the beginning of 1993, things became more difficult. Many companies proposed their alternative, usually rigged, auction procedures. One idea was to sell a small block of shares in a voucher auction to establish a price, and then sell the rest at that fixed price in a subscription. Aside from being horribly inefficient, this procedure would have enabled managers to decide to whom to sell and not to sell their company's shares.

After a couple tries in the city of Vladimir and elsewhere, this procedure was abandoned. Many regions also tried to improve on the software that GKI wrote for administering the voucher auctions, in part to make sure they had an easier time losing track of unwanted bids and in part to show their independence. This, too, went nowhere. But the biggest problems were political rather than administrative. Initially, many regions refused to conduct voucher auctions altogether, while only the most progressive ones in Siberia and in the cities around Moscow were willing to get started. In the meantime, opponents of privatization started a loud campaign against vouchers, proposing to turn them into means of payment for medical expenses and education rather than the currency of privatization. To top this off, Gaidar was removed under parliamentary pressure as prime minister in December.

Despite these setbacks, the pace of voucher auctions kept accelerating, so strong was the incentive managers had. As Table 5.1 shows, in December 1992, 18 firms were sold in 8 out of 89 possible regions. By April 1993, the pace of voucher auctions reached 614 firms in 70 regions. In May, the rate fell because auction preparations stopped in April in anticipation of the public referendum on Yeltsin's leadership. In June, sales recovered to 907 firms in 80 regions, and stayed at around 900 firms per month in the following year, with 86 regions participating. There was a surprisingly small slowdown after the election in December 1993, despite the poor showing of Gaidar's party and the success of Vladimir Zhirinovsky. When it became clear that reforms would continue, the pace of voucher auctions bounced back.

In June 1994, the last month of voucher privatization, some of the largest Russian firms came on the market, and almost 3,000 firms were privatized, accounting for over a quarter of total privatized assets. During that month, many of the most valuable companies were sold, including those in telecommunications, nonferrous metals, and oil and gas. For the first time, foreigners actively participated in voucher auctions. Not surprisingly, the voucher price soared above $20. Altogether, over 14,000 firms went through voucher auctions in 20 months, corresponding to roughly two-thirds of the qualified universe. About 97 million vouchers were accepted in these auctions (out of a total of 144 million), with almost all the rest used up in closed subscriptions and small-scale privatizations.

Another way to look at the pace of sales is by focusing on the number of employees who worked in privatized companies. As voucher privatization got going, roughly 900,000 employees were shifting from public to private payrolls each month. With the addition of 3.9 million people employed at firms privatized in June of 1994, the total added up to almost 18 million people, or two-thirds of the Russian manufacturing labor force.

In an average voucher auction, the selling firm had about 1,300 employees and sold about 18 percent of its shares. The average percentage sold is lower than the 29 percent Yeltsin decreed for two reasons. First, many strategic companies in which the government retained a controlling stake sold fewer shares. In fact, firms with more than 10,000 employees sold only 15.5 percent of their shares in voucher auctions. Second, some firms went through two voucher auctions to sell the full 29 percent that Yeltsin decreed, and the 18 percent average counts each of these auctions as a separate observation. If we could add up the shares each firm sold in all its voucher auctions, the average would have been higher than 18 percent.

In the last year of privatization, voucher auctions became an integral part of the Russian economic and social landscape. Privatization was heavily advertised by GKI on television and

Table 5.1.
Voucher auctions in Russia, December 1992–June 1994

	Dec	Jan	Feb	Mar	Apr	May	Jun	Jul	Aug	Sep
Number of enterprises sold by calendar month*	18	108	197	450	611	577	910	917	895	811
Cumulative total regions**	8	26	41	58	70	73	80	82	82	83
Enterprise charter capital, rbl. mln.	3,041	6,025	8,678	21,284	29,235	25,286	38,543	36,098	35,439	38,123
Employment, thousands	43	188	200	556	836	600	820	787	828	825
Charter capital sold, rbl. mln.	513	676	1,685	5,266	6,294	5,208	7,117	8,280	7,010	7,432
Weighted average share package sold***	16.9%	11.2%	19.4%	24.7%	21.5%	20.6%	18.5%	23.0%	19.8%	19.5%
Total vouchers accepted, thousands	158	159	611	2,284	4,147	4,331	4,364	6,828	4,489	5,089
Weighted average auction rate****	3.2	4.2	2.8	2.3	1.5	1.2	1.6	1.2	1.6	1.5

*The numbers in this row refer to voucher auctions held. Some enterprises had more than one voucher auction. As a result, the total number of firms sold in voucher auctions is lower than 15,779 and is closer to 14,000.

**Total number of regions that have held auction to date

***Weighted average percent of shares of enterprises sold

****Expresses the number of 1,000 rouble shares that are exchanged for one voucher at auction

Source: GKI/RPC Performance Database

Table 5.1.
continued

	Oct	Nov	Dec	Jan	Feb	Mar	Apr	May	Jun	Total
Number of enterprises sold by calendar month*	963	1,002	1,044	733	779	967	1,057	1,119	2,621	15,779
Cumulative total regions**	83	83	83	84	86	86	86	86	86	86
Enterprise charter capital, rbl. mln.	44,720	48,414	47,092	46,057	60,875	109,852	96,917	69,393	386,380	1,151,450
Employment, thousands	910	903	1,025	659	1,282	1,069	1,245	1,131	3,863	17,772
Charter capital sold, rbl. mln.	8,172	9,019	8,792	9,078	13,687	16,633	18,438	16,082	55,414	202,797
Weighted average share package sold***	18.3%	18.6%	18.7%	19.7%	22.5%	15.1%	17.0%	23.2%	14.3%	17.6%
Total vouchers accepted, thousands	4,617	3,158	3,543	3,151	4,550	8,969	13,620	8,805	30,735	113,587
Weighted average auction rate****	1.8	2.9	2.5	2.9	3.0	1.9	1.2	1.8	1.8	1.8

in newspapers. The slogan *privatizatsiya,* with *za* (which in Russian means "for" as opposed to "against") emblazoned in bold red letters on a blue background, appeared almost everywhere. Heavy television advertising by voucher funds added to the publicity. At some point, a popular song called "Wow, wow, voucher!" rose to number five on the Russian Hit Parade. The high point came when President Yeltsin decided that "voucher auction" was a foreign term unfit for a truly Russian program. From then on, officials had to use the term "people's subscription," by analogy with closed subscriptions for managers and workers. Needless to say, everyone continued to refer to voucher auctions as voucher auctions.

Many foreign dignitaries came to see Russian privatization in action. Brian Atwood, the head of the United States Agency for International Development, asked a woman at the Moscow Auction Center what she was buying. She explained that she was interested in the shares of a bakery that supplied her district in Moscow, and that she was planning to attend a shareholder meeting and give the management some ideas for product improvement. She also explained that her family diversified their holdings, so that, while she was buying shares of the bakery, her husband and her son were buying shares in other companies. Mr. Atwood later reported that Russia was the first place he saw where capitalism really worked.

Of course, not all auctions went equally well. Some of the largest firms used their political connections to change the rules for their auctions, usually with sorry results. For example, VAZ, the producer of heavily exported Lada cars and the largest enterprise in Russia, employing over half a million workers and accounting for 7 percent of GDP, designed its own voucher auction procedure. It also introduced a restriction that large investors could only submit bids in person by visiting the remote headquarters of the firm. Despite a blessing from Yeltsin, this voucher auction procedure did not work. But VAZ succeeded in discouraging investors. Its total market value, as implied by share prices obtained in the voucher auction, was around $45 million. To put this number in perspective, in 1991, Fiat reportedly offered the Russian government at least $2 billion for the company.

Another good example of high-level intervention in voucher auctions is Gazprom, the Russian natural gas monopoly. By restricting participation in voucher auctions to only individual investors, and excluding both foreign and professional buyers, the company came out of the voucher auction with a valuation of under $228 million, which is roughly one thousandth of the value put on it by foreign investment banks. But the best example of old guard managers in action remains GAZ, the Gorky Auto Works, which produces trucks and Volga passenger cars. The general director of the company succeeded in buying up most of the shares offered in a voucher auction using a cheap loan from the government, which was meant to save thousands of jobs at GAZ. He was surprised when GKI interceded and prevented him from bidding for government property with government money.

Nor did voucher auctions go equally well in all parts of Russia. Initially, many regions dominated by communist governments opposed the idea, although most of them later agreed to privatization of at least some firms. Similarly, some reformist regions, such as Nizhny Novgorod, initially opposed voucher auctions because their leaders claimed that they had better ways to privatize (the never-ending squabbles among reformers is one of Russia's most persistent problems). A few ethnic regions, such as Tatarstan, Kalmikiya, and Chukhotka also refused to participate, in part to show their defiance of the central government. Regions of the Russian Caucasus ravaged by civil war hardly privatized either. In some regions, such as the Far East, voucher auctions were attempted but then stopped after outside investors in some companies bought enough shares to oust the incumbent managers. The government of the region reacted by reversing privatization, and putting all regional firms into a holding company it controlled.

But perhaps the most vociferous opposition came toward the end of privatization from Moscow Mayor Yuri Luzhkov, who violently opposed voucher auctions and strongly preferred the cash sales of companies. With Yeltsin's eventual political support, Luzhkov managed to stop voucher privatization in Moscow in May of 1994, after many Moscow firms had already privatized. In describing this episode, Chubais compared himself to General Mikhail Kutuzov who gave up Moscow to Napoleon in 1812 in order to save Russia.

But what is most interesting about all these examples is that they were the exception rather than the rule. In almost all of Russia's regions, voucher auctions started early in 1993 and proceeded according to the rules at a remarkably rapid pace. Most companies, other than the largest ones, sold 29 percent of their shares in unrestricted voucher auctions. Thanks to reliance on competition and extremely streamlined bureaucratic procedures, voucher auctions were relatively incorrupt. By the end of the voucher program, over 14,000 firms employing two-thirds of the industrial labor force had been privatized. Just as impressive as this outcome is the fact that it happened during a brief yet tumultuous 20-month period of countless parliamentary battles, several cabinet shake-ups, a hotly contested referendum on economic reforms, an attempted coup, and an election that reformers lost. In his announcement of the conclusion of the voucher privatization program, Chubais observed that privatization was the first major national program in Russia since the revolution of 1917 that was completed in time and that accomplished more than it had promised.

4 The Shareholders

Who were the new owners of the Russian companies, and what exactly did they acquire in voucher auctions? We address these questions by first presenting some evidence on the ownership profiles of Russian firms, and then examining the emerging corporate governance activity.

Systematic data on management and other shareholder ownership in Russia do not exist. In 1993, two researchers working at GKI, Joseph Blasi and Katarina Pistor, conducted small surveys of firms that asked managers about the the ownership structure of their firms. The surveys asked not just about the results of voucher auctions, but also about the actual ownership structure that emerged after some initial trading of shares. Although the data in these surveys were self-reported, and hence in some cases might have been incorrect, they presented a very clear picture. In the Blasi sample of 143 medium-sized and large companies, through closed subscriptions and subsequent acquisition of shares, managers and workers together ended up owning an average of 65 percent of the shares.[1] Of that, about 8.6 percent on average was owned by the top management team. The ownership of the additional shares was divided between outsiders and the Russian government, with the outsiders owning an average of 21.5 percent and the government owning an average of 13 percent. In most cases, the government shares were earmarked for future employee purchases and investment tenders.

Despite a high level of ownership, managers surveyed by Blasi wanted to own more shares. An average general director in his sample argued that an optimal ownership structure would put 72 percent of the shares in the hands of the insiders, with 32 percent for the employees and 40 percent for top managers. An average general director also volunteered that, of the 40 percent, it would be optimal for him to have 31 percent, and for the rest of the management team to have 9 percent. The outsiders should own 27 percent, none of which should be held by the government. Consistent with their view of optimality, general directors were actively buying additional shares from the workers.

Even the existing management equity ownership underestimates the degree of their control. Indeed, managers in most companies aggressively consolidated their control by securing workers' voting support either informally or through trust arrangements, in which workers surrendered their votes to managers. In several takeover situations, managers succeeded in keeping their jobs only because workers backed them. Interestingly, with a few exceptions in which the workers backed outside investors in ousting the incumbent managers, workers have not shown much activism as shareholders. It could be that managers bought this peace by promising workers job security. This, however, does not appear to be the case. Many managers have laid off workers, put them on prolonged leave, and otherwise showed a lack of responsiveness to workers' interests. While worker passivity in Russia should calm fears of worker control, it only deepens concerns about management entrenchment.

In the Blasi sample, an average of about 21.5 percent of the shares was owned by outside investors. Of that, about 11 percent was owned by holders of blocks larger than 5 percent whom managers were willing to identify to the interviewer. The remaining shares held by outsiders were owned by individuals (4 percent) and investors, such as voucher funds, with blocks of less than 5 percent. Evidence from the largest companies suggests an even greater incidence of blockholders. Of the 30 percent of shares offered in a voucher auction of the truck maker ZIL, about 28 percent were bought by seven large investors, many of whom turned out to be affiliated with Mikrodin, a private computer trading firm. A private conglomerate called Bioprocess bought an 18 percent stake in Uralmash, a huge Siberian machine builder, as well as in dozens of other industrial firms. The investment fund Alpha Capital bought a 10 percent stake in the Bolshevik Cake Factory. CSFB bought large stakes in several companies, including LOMO, a well-known optical firm in St. Petersburg. Indeed, a core investor seems to have emerged in nearly every one of the most promising privatizations.

This evidence underscores the importance of voucher tradeability for the formation of blockholdings in Russia. To acquire large stakes in firms, investors needed to accumulate blocks of vouchers and then bid them in voucher auctions. Without voucher tradeability, only investment funds would have been able to build large stakes before the aftermarket developed. The liquid voucher market has enabled Russian privatization to do what for political reasons it could not do directly: to create core investors for many major companies.

Who are these large investors? They appear to be of three types. The first is private voucher investment funds which were created following the Czech model, and which, as we mentioned, collected 45 million vouchers. Although most Russian funds so far appear to be uninterested in corporate governance, some of the largest funds have acquired large stakes in several companies and have actively challenged management.

The second type of large investors is wealthy individuals and private firms, such as Bioprocess and Mikrodin, which made their fortunes in the last few years in trade and other commercial activities. These investors often have the financial muscle to stand up to the managers. While managers try to discourage these investors, they typically do not just go away.

The third category of large investors is foreigners. To them, the low prices in voucher auctions presented a powerful attraction. At the same time, they did not usually openly challenge the managers, for fear of a political reaction. Foreign participation in the voucher auctions played a relatively minor role until May 1994, but in the last two months of mass privatization, and shortly afterwards, over $2 billion in foreign portfolio investment entered Russia.

Anecdotal evidence suggests that large shareholders often try to use their votes to change company policies. Alpha Capital, for example, has campaigned to force firms it invested in to pay dividends. An outside investor in Vladimir Tractor Works eventually gained control of the company and installed his own management. Mikrodin succeeded in replacing the general directors of both Permsky Motors, the largest jet engine maker in Russia, and the Moscow truck maker ZIL. First Voucher, the largest voucher fund, has its representatives appointed to chair the boards of the companies in which it holds large stakes. In other cases, such as that of Uralmash, Bioprocess cooperated with the management in an aggressive restructuring program.

Large shareholder activism is beginning to show up in statistics as well. In Vladimir, Yaroslavl, and Rostov, three large Russian cities for which data are available, 10 percent of the general directors were removed at the first shareholder meeting by coalitions of outside investors and employees. While Russia sorely needs even faster turnover of the old guard managers, the existing pace is already impressive. Large shareholders are clearly pushing companies toward efficient ownership structures in which cash flow and control rights are effectively lined up.

Not all managers have acquiesced. In some cases where workers are selling shares to outsiders, managers have threatened them with dismissal. Some managers physically threaten challengers at shareholder meetings, rig shareholder votes, illegally change corporate charters (from one-share-one-vote to one-shareholder-one-vote), refuse to record share trades in corporate share registers, and so on. In many cases, these strategies succeed in stopping control challenges from outside investors.

Many managers are also appealing to politicians to restrain large investors. Right after the voucher auction, the manager of Bolshevik Cake Factory unsuccessfully lobbied GKI to force Alpha Capital, the large investor, to sell its shares. Several local governments have intervened to force blockholders to sell their shares. And in perhaps the most daring action so far, the director of ZIL, who was subsequently removed, publicly appealed to Yeltsin to maintain the government's control of the company through a so-called golden share, thus eliminating the controlling influence of Mikrodin. Yet despite these attempts, political interference in most cases has failed to prevent outside investors from exercising meaningful control.

Over time, the role of the large shareholders in corporate governance is only likely to increase. In the summer and fall of 1994, as the market values of shares of privatized firms began to rise, workers sharply accelerated the pace of selling their shares. Outside the gates of many companies, it is common to see a bus which serves as a buying point of workers' shares. In most cases, these shares are bought by brokers for large investors. Managers are buying shares from the workers as well, but in many cases outsiders are getting more. By some estimates, workers have already sold a quarter of the shares distributed to them. If outsiders succeed in getting a significant fraction of workers' shares, their role in corporate governance will increase dramatically.

The other substantial opportunity for outside investors to gain more control is investment tenders, in which the government sells its residual 15 to 20 percent equity stake in exchange for a commitment to future investment in the company. Despite a slow start in 1994, the pace of investment tenders had accelerated by the time privatization ended, largely because subsidized credits got harder to come by and firms needed funds. Many of these investment tenders have been tainted, as the managers accepted less capital from investors who did not challenge their control. For example, the winner of the investment tender for Lada car maker VAZ was AVVA, the dubious financial group controlled by VAZ itself. Not surprisingly, AVVA received the stake for the reserve price, and there were no competitors. Despite the common occurrence of such corruption, many managers choose to give up some control in exchange for capital and know-how, which bodes well for the future of corporate governance. In market economies as well, managers typically give up control only in exchange for capital.

In sum, the ownership structure of Russian firms has taken a giant leap toward efficiency as a result of privatization. The government has sold most of its shares in the process, and most of the rest have been allocated to workers and to investment tenders. Political control through share ownership has largely disappeared. The managers emerged from privatization with large share ownership, which gave them considerable interest in maximizing profits. Most large companies have obtained block investors, who are in many cases pushing the managers toward restructuring, or even replacing the managers. At the same time, managers often have control rights out of proportion with their cash flow claims, and use these rights to keep themselves at the helm, a policy that is usually inconsistent with efficiency. These managers are also tied to politicians through a system of subsidies and government orders. The evidence from shareholdings suggests that the ownership structure in Russia is not fully efficient, but is moving in the right direction.

5 Asset Values

One of the most conspicuous results of voucher auctions is the low prices that companies fetched. A rough calculation enables us to value Russian industry. About 100 million vouchers were accepted in the voucher auctions, and they bought about 18 percent of Russian industry. Over the 20 months of privatization, the price of the voucher fluctuated between $4 in the winter of 1993 and around $20 in June of 1994. For most privatized firms, the voucher price was not higher than $20. Under this assumption, the implied aggregate value of the Russian industry was under $12 billion. That is, the equity of all of the Russian industry, including oil, gas, some transportation and most of manufacturing, was worth less than that of Kellogg or Anheuser-Busch. The Russian voucher privatization was, as the *Economist* called it, "the sale of the century."[2]

Perhaps an even more dramatic way to look at the numbers is to examine the prices in some key voucher auctions. To put dollar values on a company sold in a voucher auction, we use the approximate price of the voucher at the time the relevant auction was completed, and combine it with the information on the number of vouchers accepted and the percentage of the company privatized in the auction. The largest privatized firm in Russia in terms of employment was VAZ, a company which effectively rigged its voucher auction and obtained a valuation of only $45 million. The second largest firm, with over 200,000 employees, was United Energy Systems, the utility that owns most of Russia's power plants. At $647 million, it achieved the highest implied market value of any firm sold in a voucher auction, largely because of significant foreign participation in its auction. Still, the replacement cost of this company's assets is probably much higher. The third largest company is Norilsk Nickel, which produces a significant share of the world's nickel yet had an implied market capitalization of under $500 million.

An even more dramatic way to see the low valuations is to focus on some large manufacturing companies. The market value of ZIL, the truck and limousine maker with 100,000 employees, was about $16 million. The market value of GAZ, a giant automobile and truck manufacturer, was $27 million. Russia's largest steelworks had a market value of $47 million. A tractor factory with 54,000 employees had an implied market value of $2.3 million, and a steelworks with 45,000 employees had a market value of $5.5 million. The market values of two household names in Russian manufacturing, Uralmash and Permsky Motors, were $4 million and $6 million respectively.

One way to put these numbers in context is to note that U.S. manufacturing companies have market values of about $100,000 per employee. Russian manufacturing companies, in contrast, obtained voucher auction values of between $100 and $500 per employee. The difference is about 200-fold! Indeed, a value of $20 billion for a Western automobile company comparable in size to VAZ, or of $4 billion for a counterpart of Uralmash, is plausible. When we first made this calculation in the middle of 1993, before later privatizations fetched higher prices, the ratio was not 200, but 1,000![3] What might explain such low prices of Russian assets?

One hypothesis is that most of these firms are so inefficient that they are actually worthless. Yet that goes only part of the way in explaining the valuations. Consider the following rough calculation. Estimates of the Russian standard of living typically put it at about one-tenth of the Western standard. If the value of companies were in the same proportion to wages in Russia as in the West, then these Russian companies should be worth about one-tenth of what their Western counterparts are worth. On this calculation, the value ratio of 200 still seems too high by a factor of 20.

Another hypothesis attributes the low value of assets to the low level of private wealth in Russia, which translates into the low price of the voucher. This capital shortage theory is not entirely persuasive since there was perhaps $15 billion of capital flight from Russia in 1992. Moreover, foreigners could participate in voucher auctions, and did so very actively in the summer of 1994, when asset prices, while rising from 1993 levels, remained very low. Even when foreigners participated, the voucher price rose to only about $20, which we used to compute the $12 billion valuation of Russian industry. Nonetheless, there probably is some truth to this theory. In the summer of 1994, the shares of some privatized companies began actively trading in Russia, with prices of some stocks, especially in the oil industry, rising as much as tenfold. The stock market boom was driven by foreign portfolio investment as well as the large accumulation of domestic savings in 1994, which suggested that undervaluation in voucher auctions might have resulted from capital shortage. At the same time, even the high-flying oil stocks remained 20 to 30 times cheaper per barrel of reserves than their Western counterparts. Despite the stock market rise, valuations remained very low.

The most plausible explanation for Russian industry's low valuation lies in the theory of inefficient ownership and the misalignment of cash flow and control rights. Voucher auction prices reflected the values of the companies to outside investors, who received legal cash flow rights but, as we argued above, relatively few control rights. The control rights were held primarily by managers, who had an interest in value maximization because of their high ownership stakes, but had other interests as well.

The problem of managers simply diverting assets for their own use has not disappeared, although it has been reduced by privatization. In addition, to consolidate control against potential interference by outside investors, some managers cater to the workers who still own the majority of shares. Many Russian firms continue to pay for housing, child care, hospitals, schools and other services for their employees, a practice that is likely to continue unless managers stop needing worker support, or unless a better social safety net is provided by the government. When managers and workers join together to spend the profits of a company they control, outside investors are unlikely to have much left over. Perhaps most importantly, many companies are stuck with managers who lack the knowledge and ability to carry out restructuring, but who value their jobs too highly to leave despite their high ownership. A recent empirical study of privatized shops in Russia showed that a change of owners and managers is a better predictor of actual restructuring of shops than is the provision of ownership incentives to the old managers.[4] The study is at least suggestive that old human capital holds back industrial firms as well.

Still, managerial discretion is probably not the whole explanation for the low valuation, since such problems also often exist in the West in a milder form. The low valuations suggest that the depoliticization of Russian firms has not been complete, and politicians maintain extensive control over companies. Even with sectoral ministries out of the picture, residual control enables politicians to expropriate shareholder wealth through regulations, restrictions on product mix and layoffs, custom duties and many other interventions, including the threat of potential nationalization. Continued politicization is surely the main reason that outside investors pay so little for Russian assets.

6 Summary

In many ways, privatization radically changed the Russian economy. Yet a serious assessment of the program requires that we answer the tough question: how substantive have these changes been? After all, most of Russian agriculture has experienced a legal transformation as well, whereby collective farms were transformed into closed partnerships owned by their workers, but little has changed in the way it functions. Since we argued that the main cause of inefficiency under socialism is inefficient ownership, the first place to evaluate privatization is ownership changes. The main yardstick of good reform we have set out in this regard is depoliticization. The second yardstick is corporate governance.

The principal accomplishment of privatization has been the massive retreat of the government from economic activity, and the transfer of control rights from politicians to managers and investors. The sectoral ministries, which only two years ago were still making decisions for firms from Moscow, have faded into irrelevance and obscurity. Managers are deciding who they do business with and how, including major decisions about asset sales, mergers, and joint ventures, without consulting their former ministries. The extent of depoliticization of Russian firms has been extremely significant.

However, the process is incomplete. Politicians still influence firms through multiple levers. The most important one is centralized credit policies, whereby firms get cheap credits to maintain employment and output. Moreover, in many cases where the central government has reduced its control over firms, local governments have stepped in and increased theirs, largely because social services continue to be provided through firms. And despite privatization, the Russian economy remains one of the most regulated in the world, in which taxes are arbitrary and industry-specific, foreign trade is heavily controlled through licensing, employment policies are governed by a myriad of prohibitions, anti-monopoly policy is unpredictable, and many real estate transactions are rendered impossible by legal restrictions on transfers of land.

Firms emerged from privatization in a situation where managers had the preponderance of control rights as well as substantial, though not complete, cash flow rights. In many cases, this gave managers incentives to restructure themselves as well as to listen to outside investors proposing restructuring plans, which made these companies very different from collective farms and shops with no outside investors to pressure for change. In other cases, even after privatization, managers pursued objectives other than maximization of their wealth as stockholders, and turned to self-dealing, diversion of company profits, and, perhaps most important, retention of their own jobs. This behavior, however, increasingly is being challenged by outside investors. And no matter how problematic, managerial abuse of control creates far fewer obstacles to efficiency than political abuse of control.

In 1991, the Russian government was unsure whether privatization was a suitable alternative to political control, with all its inefficiencies. Few people had faith that a privatization program, even if adopted, could be implemented on a significant scale. Serious people proposed privatizing, and restructuring, just a few dozen firms. Only three years later, tens of thousands of firms of all sizes had been privatized, Russia had 40 million shareholders, the politicians were in rapid retreat, and many firms had begun to restructure on their own. The very fact that continued deregulation and corporate governance in the Russian economy became the new issues for debate is in itself an eloquent testimony of privatization's extraordinary success.

Notes

1. Joseph Blasi (1994), "Ownership, Governance and Restructuring," manuscript, New Jersey: Rutgers University School of Management and Labor Relations.

2. *The Economist*, "Sale of the Century," CCCXXXI (14 May 1994), 67–69.

3. Maxim Boycko, Andrei Shleifer and Robert W. Vishny (1993), "Privatizing Russia," *Brookings Papers on Economic Activity II*, 139–181.

4. Nicholas Barberis, Maxim Boycko, Andrei Shleifer and Natalia Tsukanova (1994), "How Does Privatization Work? Evidence from the Russian Shops," manuscript, Harvard University.

6

From Privatization to Restructuring

In chapter 5, we showed how Russian privatization began the process of depoliticizing firms and introducing effective corporate governance—the two critical elements of efficient ownership. Yet improving the ownership structure is only a means to an end. The ultimate goal is efficient performance of privatized firms. To accomplish this, most Russian firms need a radical restructuring of their operations, covering such diverse areas as new products, internal reorganization, financial management, sales and marketing, and production technologies. Since mass privatization is barely finished, for most firms this process has just begun. The speed and the scope of restructuring will ultimately determine the success of privatization.

It is not enough to expect widespread restructuring to occur simply because firms are now private. Indeed, since restructuring often calls for employment cutbacks, changes in product lines (often away from defense), joint ventures with foreign investors, and cuts in social spending on employees, politicians often oppose it. To promote restructuring, post-privatization reforms must accelerate depoliticization of Russian firms.

On the corporate governance front, many problems remain as well. Most of the old guard managers have kept their jobs, and are still seeking government handouts to continue doing business as usual. Despite the incentives coming from cash flow ownership, these managers usually lack the necessary human capital to undertake radical restructuring measures, such as skills to launch marketing and sales programs. These directors are good at getting subsidies and supplies, not at making and selling good products. The obsolescence of human capital at the helm of privatized firms is the most significant cost of deficient corporate governance.

To stimulate restructuring, free-market reformers must pursue efforts to take the remaining control rights away from politicians and allocate them to private agents who have the corresponding cash flow rights. At the same time, they must continue efforts to reallocate control rights from managers to outside investors. In many cases, control by investors relies on protection of contracts between them and the firms. The next stage of reforms needs not only to continue improving the ownership structure, but also to focus on contract enforcement and protection of property, for which private owners now have a demand. In this chapter, we describe several near-term post-privatization reforms that can move Russia toward a better property rights system and thereby stimulate restructuring.

First, firms must be encouraged to shift from public to private means of raising capital. This would both deprive politicians of their principal mechanism of influencing firms, namely subsidies and cheap credits, and stimulate corporate governance by private capital providers. Although privatization has created a strong momentum toward the development of private securities markets and capital provision more generally, genuine progress in this area is possible only when the government stops supplying capital. As we show below, this would only occur under macroeconomic stabilization.

Second, urban real estate must be privatized. During privatization, it became clear that public ownership of real estate was a key source of income for local officials, who exercised their control over real estate by demanding bribes and kickbacks. Turning urban real estate over to private investors can cut the power of local politicians over firms, as well as give these firms access to capital from real estate sales.

Third, the government needs an aggressive competition policy. In market economies, active product market competition is the most effective corporate governance mechanism, since firms facing such competition must be efficient to survive, and in particular cannot afford to keep bad management. Product market competition also makes it harder for politicians to control firms.

Finally, social assets currently maintained by firms must be transferred to local governments. As both a financial burden on firms and an excuse for political interference, enterprise ownership of social assets has slowed restructuring. We describe a mechanism for transferring social assets.

None of these post-privatization reforms, however, can be fully effective without wholesale reform of the legal system to ensure contract enforcement and protection of property. Private capital provision, real estate deals, and many other transactions in a private economy depend on this key element of well-established property rights. Here especially, Russia badly needs progress.

The reforms we describe can bring Russian firms a good deal closer to well-defined property rights, and hence to effective restructuring. At the same time, like privatization, all these reforms have opponents, ranging from many old guard managers to politicians who stand to lose control. None of these reforms is assured of success.

A good reason to be optimistic, however, is that privatization has created extensive private interests that stand to benefit from these reforms. Many managers, businessmen, financial market participants, and Russia's 40 million new shareholders, have become effective advocates of reforms. In this way, privatization has created a new reform constituency. To illustrate, Chubais once explained to us the evolution of managerial thinking. In 1991, enterprise managers came to him to lobby for inputs, such as cement. In 1992 and 1993, after price liberalization, they came to lobby for cheap credits. In 1994, after privatization, they started coming to lobby for favorable disposition of residual government shares and help with the foreign investors. The new economic interests engendered by privatization significantly improve the odds that the post-privatization reforms, and subsequent restructuring, will actually take place.

Just as with privatization, free-market reformers can use all the help they can get, including foreign aid. Since it is always limited, foreign aid cannot and should not be expected to have a significant direct impact on the economy of the country receiving assistance. Rather, foreign aid should be narrowly targeted to alter the balance of power between reformers and their opponents, so as to raise the likelihood of reforms. As we argue at the end of this chapter, United States assistance to the Russian privatization has shown how to do this effectively.

1 Restructuring

As privatization creates a more efficient ownership structure, firms should begin to make decisions that benefit wealth-maximizing shareholders, rather than politicians or entrenched managers. This should change the way they do business away from the pervasive distortions resulting from political control. Such changes are referred to as restructuring.

Restructuring capable of making formerly socialist firms efficient in a market economy has to be radical. It involves major changes in the general strategy, such as a switch from military to civilian production, or even conversion from manufacturing to services, as in the case of a major machine building firm in St. Petersburg that hopes to turn itself into a port facility. Restructuring entails substantial change in the internal organization of the firm, including the introduction of such capitalist activities as sales, marketing, and financial management, and the de-emphasis of more socialist activities, such as supply procurement and personnel indoctrination. Radical restructuring also typically calls for a significant change in operations, including large employment cutbacks and the upgrading of capital stock.

The two principal inputs into radical restructuring are human and physical capital. Unfortunately, neither of them is readily available. The old managers typically lack the skills to become capitalist directors, but are reluctant to cede their positions to people with better skills. And since politicians have long controlled the supply of physical capital, private capital has stayed out. Private physical capital will come to firms in earnest only when it can get its fair return without expropriation by politicians or managers.

Following privatization, Russian firms have slowly begun to restructure. An early survey of Russian industrial firms found that over 60 percent are taking restructuring steps, including product changes, initiation of marketing campaigns, supplier changes, and employment reductions.[1] A few showcases of more radical restructuring exist as well. For example, the St. Petersburg optical manufacturer LOMO, with the help of an

American consulting firm McKinsey, has reorganized itself into divisions, expanded production of profitable products and reduced that of unprofitable ones, reduced the labor force by a third, and created its first sales force. Several foreign investors have initiated joint ventures with the company. Similarly, Uralmash, the Siberian heavy machinery manufacturer, has over the last three years reduced its labor force from 70,000 to 20,000, and has started several joint ventures. In October of 1994, one of the U.S. government-sponsored investment funds operating in Russia announced a significant investment in one of these joint ventures. Still, such radical restructuring is not typical. Many large Russian firms have done nothing at all since privatization. In the next few sections, we describe what can be done to accelerate the pace of restructuring.

2 Raising Capital

For most companies, restructuring depends on new capital investment, which can vary from relatively small amounts needed for working capital or completion of construction projects to hundreds of millions of dollars for rehabilitation of oil wells. Whatever the requirements, capital allocation has to be apolitical. When politicians make capital allocation decisions, they usually demand that the firm produce politically desirable goods, sell them to politically desirable customers, and maintain a politically desirable level of employment. This must change.

An apolitical capital allocation system would also enhance corporate governance. Even in market economies, managers typically give up control rights and allow external scrutiny only in exchange for capital. Insiders lose control not in takeovers or proxy fights, but when the firm needs money to survive and comes to the capital market to get it. The same will happen in Russia. The old directors will lose control only when capital suppliers demand it. A private capital allocation system would thus promote depoliticization, corporate governance, and restructuring.

Even during recent reforms, most capital allocation in Russia remained heavily politicized. Firms continued to receive most of their credits through the central bank, and often paid interest on these credits out of government subsidies they received from the national budget. Loans were repaid with proceeds from new loans. In 1992, government subsidies and central bank credits together added up to over 40 percent of the GDP.[2] Agriculture and energy benefited the most from the central bank's credit policies. Not surprisingly, neither of these sectors has restructured. Although industrial, and particularly military, firms were not treated as generously, many of them still received substantial transfers. In its allocation of credits and subsidies, the government evidently did not discriminate between state and privatized firms. According to a deputy governor of the central bank, a firm applying to the government's Credit Commission for help needed to fill out a long questionnaire, which did not ask whether the firm was privatized or not.

Following the 1993 election, the Chernomyrdin government sharply reduced cheap credits and subsidies, particularly to the military-industrial sector, although transfers to agriculture and energy continued. Because of fewer credits, inflation fell from over 20 percent a month in 1993 to around 5 percent a month in late summer of 1994. To support Chernomyrdin, with whom he got along better than with the reformers Gaidar and Fyodorov, the central bank governor Gerashchenko raised real interest rates to positive levels, and demanded repayment of loans. The Chernomyrdin stabilization cut off many industrial firms from government assistance. While complaining loudly, the managers also began to look to private markets for capital. Macroeconomic discipline during this period gave a tremendous boost to private capital markets in Russia.

In 1994, stabilization depoliticized the allocation of capital through three major channels. First, the tightening of monetary policy both reduced the overall volume of cheap credits and rationalized the rules used in allocating them. The politicians' ability to distribute cheap credits to firms at their discretion was severely curtailed. Except in the highly favored sectors, such as agriculture, only the most powerful and politically visible firms, often with political ties to the President, received special subsidies in the first half of 1994. Second, stabilization raised the supply of private investment funds by encouraging domestic savings and facilitating foreign capital inflow, including the return of flight capital. By some estimates, the Russian economy generated $20 billion of new savings available for investment in the first half of 1994. Third, stabilization turned the attention of managers from cheap government credits to sources of private funds. While some managers proved incapable of changing their focus, and kept visiting Moscow officials asking for help (Chubais ascribed this to inertia), other managers looked for private loans, foreign partners and opportunities for placing equity.

Stabilization stimulated a variety of mechanisms of private capital allocation. It accelerated the rate of investment tenders, in which firms received investment commitments from core investors in return for the government's residual equity stake of 15 to 20 percent. The opportunity to get substantial stakes attracted both foreign and Russian investors to these tenders.

Unfortunately, investment tenders are often rigged, which keeps them from becoming an effective mechanism for raising capital by privatized firms.

A second mechanism for raising capital is issuing new equity to dispersed investors. Many companies are pursuing this option, in part because it threatens managers the least. The leader in this movement is LUKoil, a giant oil firm that hopes to raise millions of dollars in the West. The odds of successful equity issues greatly improved in August and September of 1994, as the Russian stock market posted impressive gains.

The demand by firms for placing equity capital has stimulated many beneficial reforms in the Russian capital market. To part with their capital, potential investors need to have an enforceable contract with the firm that assures them that their investment will not be simply expropriated by managers and workers. At a minimum, potential investors insist on information disclosure, a transparent share register, and the absence of restrictions on trading stocks. In response, Russian firms interested in issuing equity have disclosed more about themselves and supported the creation of a securities market infrastructure. Longer term, to protect their money, potential investors demand a legal and regulatory structure governing securities market participants. They have supported, both economically and politically, the creation of an independent Securities and Exchange Commission. The growth of the Russian stock market shows how reforms propagate through both economic and political channels.

Not surprisingly, many politicians interested in maintaining control over firms through the allocation of capital have not viewed the private securities market with favor. The central bank and the Ministry of Finance have made numerous attempts to control it. The central bank has repeatedly pushed the idea of organizing the market around a central physical location, which it volunteered to supply free of charge, and which would have enabled it to control capital allocation by determining the rules of share trading. Fortunately, the stock market has instead developed as a self-regulating organization of brokers and dealers, which is much less subject to overt political interference than a physical exchange. In another stab at political control, the Ministry of Finance attempted to regulate the stock market through its notoriously corrupt Tax Inspectorate, which would have probably destroyed the market. The pretext was the widely publicized collapse of the MMM financial pyramid, which actually had no relation to the market in shares of privatized firms, since MMM used its own network of brokers. In response to this political threat, Russia's new stock brokers convinced Yeltsin and Chernomyrdin not to allow the tax police to regulate the stock market. It remains to be seen whether the Russian stock market will be successfully regulated by an independent commission that can protect it from other government agencies.

The third method of raising private capital is through the banks. The Russian banks have not been a major force in providing private capital to firms. Until 1994, commercial banks made a lot of money serving as conduits for cheap credits from the central bank to firms. Some of these banks were spun off from government banks explicitly to channel credits to firms, while others were established by firms to ensure that they themselves received central bank credits. Recognizing the source of their profits, banks made loans respecting the political wishes of the central bank, and had little economic incentive for additional private lending.

In 1994, as cheap credits dried up, firms gained more interest in bank loans, and banks needed new things to do. Even so, the role of the banks as arms-length lenders to firms remained limited. A significant part of the problem was the weakness of bankruptcy regulations, which vested control over bankrupt firms in a government agency rather than with creditors. In response to this problem, banks, like other investors, have shown more interest in providing capital in exchange for equity, which gives them voting rights, than in making loans, which give them no clear control rights even when a borrower defaults. Some banks have actively participated in investment tenders, others have accumulated blocks of shares on the secondary market and sought control. The establishment of equity voting as a shareholder right is an important legacy of privatization, which has turned share voting into a viable corporate governance mechanism.

Private capital is already undermining political influence over firms. The sectoral ministries faded away when they lost the ability to allocate capital; other agencies are likely to follow. The new private capital suppliers, meanwhile, demand and often get profit maximization from firms. Private capital markets will eventually give restructuring a major boost.

As yet, these gains are not secure. The viability of private capital provision depends on the elimination of government subsidies and credits. Although Chernomyrdin made much progress in this area in the first half of 1994, in late summer central bank credits again poured out. When inflation rose as a consequence, the ruble collapsed in October and central bank governor Gerashchenko finally resigned. Stabilization remains the critical challenge of Russian reforms. The development of private capital markets, as well as many other benefits of a market economy, turn on its success.

3 Urban Land and Real Estate

Privatization of urban land and real estate are critical to re-structuring for two reasons. First, land and buildings are typically complementary to plant and equipment, which in many cases have been privatized. Until land and buildings are held privately as well, control rights over complementary assets are split between local politicians and managers, which leads to a clearly inefficient ownership structure. Politicians can and do use their control of real estate to direct managers to pursue political objectives. Managers who do not respond to politicians' requests are kicked off their premises. Second, privatization of land and real estate can provide firms with a significant source of capital for restructuring. Privatized firms often have surplus land and buildings they can easily sell. In many cases, land is their most valuable asset, which can bring a lot more money than any other means of raising capital. Real estate can also be used as collateral, which can help firms get loans.

Not surprisingly, local politicians have tried hard to keep control of urban land and real estate. In the case of small-scale privatization, local governments have insisted on leasing rather than selling publicly owned buildings and land, even when privatizing the shops that occupied them. The vagueness of lease contracts offered individual bureaucrats both power over businesses and a steady source of income from bribes. Similarly, local bureaucrats have used control over land to influence privatized industrial firms, insisting that they continue to pay for social services and maintain employment. Because it serves local governments so well, politicization of urban land and real estate persists, and slows down the restructuring of old firms and the creation of new ones.

Although urban land and real estate privatization cuts into politicians' rents, momentum is building to turn over more real estate to private owners. Privatized firms themselves are politically powerful enough to lobby for the right to get badly needed revenues through real estate sales. Entrepreneurs running new businesses are lobbying for the right to buy real estate. And local governments, badly in need of revenues, are beginning to see the benefits of selling real estate they own, and then taxing what they sell. The most effective way to give these governments a final push to sell land is to stabilize the macroeconomy, since tight money would galvanize their interest in new revenue sources. For real estate reform as well, stabilization is crucial.

4 Competition Policy

Throughout the world, product market competition is the principal driving force behind restructuring. When firms face efficient rivals, they have to become efficient themselves to survive or else they have to receive large state subsidies. Keeping an inefficient firm alive in a competitive market is much more expensive to a politician than keeping afloat a wasteful monopoly, which can pass its waste along in the form of higher prices. Since politicians realize that competition raises their cost of political influence, they often restrict it by protecting firms from both domestic and foreign rivals. The bankruptcy procedure is also often politicized, and hence inefficient firms are "rehabilitated" rather than allowed to go bankrupt. Since restriction of competition facilitates political control of firms, promoting competition is an essential part of depoliticization, as well as of restructuring.

Russia inherited from socialism a very uncompetitive economy.[3] To facilitate central control, most industries were con-
centrated. Imports stayed low, and fell further with the collapse
of the East European trade. Central planners established rigid
supply chains, and built a transportation and storage system
to match them. As a result, most firms, even if they were not
the sole producers of particular goods, had little choice but to
buy their inputs from specifically designated suppliers, and to
sell them to specifically designated customers. In the short run,
the system was designed in a way that sharply limited product
market competition.

In a desperate attempt to retain political control of the economy, over the last two years politicians tried to restrict competition even further. The central government imposed multiple
foreign trade barriers, including tariffs and quotas. Local governments put up many administrative barriers to interregional
trade, and explicitly approved several price-fixing agreements.
Both the central and the local governments instituted licensing
requirements that greatly handicap entry, including in one case
giving a local monopolist the right to license potential competitors. Perhaps the greatest danger is posed by industry associations and industrial holding companies. These politically-
created cartels are allegedly fashioned after the Japanese
keiretsu, but actually are designed to monopolize their industries and extract credits from the central government. Although
GKI has successfully resisted the creation of most of these
cartels, they have strong political support. To the extent that
Russia has an active competition policy, this policy is often
anti- rather than pro-competitive.

But even in this area, there are signs of progress. The Federal
Anti-Monopoly Agency has realized that consumer groups and
small businesses both suffer from monopolistic abuses and

hence are its natural constituencies. The agency scrapped its all-encompassing list of monopolies and opposed price-fixing agreements. It also developed a natural monopoly law, whose key contribution was to clarify that not all large firms are naturally monopolies. Although the odds are against it, the agency could play a role in reducing political influence on firms, and thus encourage restructuring.

Competition is more likely to come not from a proactive anti-monopoly policy, but rather from the inability of the government to intervene in the market and restrict entry. Although often not recorded in official statistics, private businesses are forming and growing rapidly in Russia. Imports, especially of consumer goods, are growing as well. Both new entrants and imports put competitive pressure on privatized firms. If these trends are not reversed by government policy, Russia will have genuine product market competition as well as restructuring.

5 Social Assets

A significant deterrent to enterprise restructuring in Russia is company financing of the social safety net. The majority of social services, including housing, child care, and recreation facilities are provided by firms to their employees free or below cost. By one estimate, the cost of social assets represents between 5 and 25 percent of total labor cost; by another, it eats up 80 percent of profits on average.[4] These costs do not include the often substantial commitment of management time. Even unemployment insurance is effectively paid by firms, which keep workers on long-term leaves at low wages rather than lay them off. Workers now typically rely on their firms for much of both their income and consumption, whether or not they are in fact productively employed by the firms.

By far the largest expense is subsidized housing, which covers over half of total social asset costs. The second largest expense is child care, which takes up between a quarter and a third of the total social expenditure of firms. In 1993, it cost about 25,000 rubles a month to support one child in daycare, which amounted to almost half of an industrial worker's salary.[5] But parents paid only between 5 and 20 percent of the cost, and the rest was paid by firms. As a result, many privatized firms found the maintenance of daycare centers to be too expensive and have been closing them down and leasing out the space to commercial firms. The number of such centers in Russia has fallen, although demand is falling also because of declining birth rates.

Company financing of social services links firms closer with local governments, which subsidize them in exchange for continued social spending. This dependence on local governments only maintains politicization of firms and postpones restructuring. In some cases, a firm cannot go bankrupt, since, if it does, its employees lose not only jobs but also housing, child care, and recreation. The social obligations of firms essentially rule out liquidation, as opposed to rehabilitation, as a viable bankruptcy procedure. The social asset commitments also make firms unattractive investment candidates, especially to foreign investors who fear political retribution if they cut these expenditures. This is yet another example of politicization shutting off private capital supply. Company financing is an inefficient means of maintaining social services.

Privatization did not solve this problem. In the program, firms were given the option to transfer their social assets to the local government, if the latter agreed to take them. In some cases, local governments have accepted responsibility for social services, but the majority refused. Most social assets remain financed by the now-privatized firms.

The transfer of social assets to local governments remains a top priority. By depoliticizing firms, this transfer can speed up the restructuring of privatized firms, including the bankruptcy of the truly nonviable ones. Although in 1993 managers might have needed to hold on to social assets as chips in the bargaining for credits, cuts in available subsidies have eliminated this need. In fact, managers of privatized firms have lobbied for, rather than against, the transfer of social assets.

How might local governments be convinced to take these assets? Although they could in principle finance the cost of maintaining social assets with taxes and user fees, localities are unlikely to jump at the opportunity to assume this additional responsibility. To raise funds, they are also certain to lobby the central government for subsidies. This is Russian-style fiscal federalism, in which local governments, by threatening separatism and social unrest, extract resources from Moscow, which finances the expenditure by printing money.[6]

In this situation, one mechanism for convincing the local governments to accept social assets is transitional financing with foreign aid. Resources for this purpose were made available in the G-7 assistance package allocated to Russia at the 1993 Tokyo summit. With the support of the World Bank, the Russian Privatization Center started a $20 million pilot project to support the transfer of daycare centers to local governments in several regions of Russia. The funds will subsidize the transfer of daycare to the local governments over a two-year period. A $20 million budget can take care of about 50,000 children, and perhaps pave the way for broader programs of divesting social assets.

6 Foreign Aid

Few subjects in the discussion of Russian reforms arouse as much controversy as foreign aid. Western donors complain of not having enough money to be generous, especially given social problems they face at home. Newspapers publish vivid accounts of the high fees and luxurious living of Western consultants in Moscow, which promptly outrage voters and lawmakers. Even the Russians themselves complain that aid goes to Western contractors rather than to the Russians.

Most of these criticisms are misplaced. Western governments give aid to Russia not because they are charitable, but because their own national security interests demand a stable and peaceful transition from communism. Economic aid to Russia is probably the least expensive and most effective form of defense spending by either the United States or Western Europe. Western consultants, while not engaging in charity, bring many necessary technical skills. It is true that Peace Corps volunteers are more idealistic and enthusiastic, as well as less expensive, than professional consultants, but they are also less skilled. Finally, simply giving cash to Russian organizations is not always the best aid strategy, especially if the donor cares to find out how the cash was spent.

Although the criticisms of aid are exaggerated, there is a genuine issue of how to make it more effective. The United States assistance to the Russian privatization through the U.S. Agency for International Development is an example of a successful aid program, from which some general lessons can be learned. Starting in late 1992, U.S.A.I.D. financed technical assistance to privatization. It financed the development of the National Auction System, which enabled people all over Russia to bid for shares in privatizing companies. It sent professionals into various regions to help run voucher auctions. It funded a national education campaign that made the public aware of privatization. It funded several technical procedures, such as cancellation of vouchers after they were used to pay for shares. At the later stages, U.S.A.I.D. moved to technical assistance with land registration, securities markets, enterprise restructuring and legal reform. There is no doubt that American technical assistance vastly improved the quality and the speed of Russian privatization. In the first two years, the total cost of this program was around $120 million. Since, as we argue in this book, privatization fundamentally transformed the Russian economy, this money delivered good results.

We see a clear lesson in this experience. Aid cannot be used directly to restructure the Russian economy: that would simply require too much money and time. Unless provided on a truly massive scale, aid cannot directly change the economic equilibrium. However, aid can change the political equilibrium by explicitly helping free-market reformers to defeat their opponents. As we argued in Chapter 3, market reformers always face massive opposition from the traditional politicians and other interest groups when they begin to depoliticize the economy. Aid can help reformers by paying for the design and implementation of their projects, which gives them a greater capacity for action than their opponents have. Aid helps reform not because it directly helps the economy—it is simply too small for that—but because it helps the reformers in their political battles. To be effective, aid simply has to be political.

In 1992 and 1993, the United States government used its assistance funds to support the policies of Gaidar and Chubais. The assistance paid for programs that would not have been financed by the conservative Parliament, and thus allowed these programs to go ahead. The U.S. government did not spend much time in those years on projects with anti-reformers. It did not provide funds to keep state firms afloat. It did not give money to the Parliament or to reactionary agencies. Such programs could have been easily justified if the idea was to put resources into the Russian economy rather than to spur reform. After all, as the World Bank has long known, there is nothing easier than giving a government a subsidized loan to support state firms. Such loans might (though usually do not) help the economy even if they delay reforms, and are therefore eagerly accepted by most ministries. In contrast, U.S. aid to Russia worked because it was given to reformers to pursue reforms, and hence gave them the advantage of both resources and know-how over their opponents. The success of post-privatization reforms described in this chapter is also likely to depend on continuation of such political aid from the U.S. and other Western governments.

Notes

1. Leila Webster, et al. (1994), "Newly Privatized Enterprises: A Survey," in *Russia: Creating Private Enterprises and Efficient Markets,* eds. Ira Lieberman and John Nellis, Washington, D.C.: The World Bank, Private Sector Development Department.

2. World Bank (1993), "Russia: The Banking System in Transition," unpublished paper, Agriculture, Industry, and Finance Division, Country Department III, Europe and Central Asia Region (May 26); and "Subsidies and Directed Credits to Enterprises in Russia: A Strategy for Reform," unpublished paper, Country Operations Division 2, ECA Country Department III (April 8).

3. The best description of the Russian industrial organization and the emerging competition policy is contained in Paul Joskow, Richard Schmalensee and Natalia Tsukanova (1994), "Competitive Policy in Russia during and after Privatization," *Brookings Papers on Economic Activity: Microeconomics,* 301–375.

4. Evgeny Yasin (1994), "Conception of the Separation of the Social Sphere of the Enterprises," paper prepared for Prime Minister Chernomyrdin.

5. Alexander Bim (1994), study prepared for the Russian Privatization Center, Moscow.

6. Daniel Triesman (1994), "Fiscal Federalism in Post-Communist Russia," chapter III of *The Politics of Fiscal Redistribution in Post-Communist Russia,* unpublished Ph.D. dissertation, Cambridge: Harvard University, presents remarkable evidence showing that Russia's separatist regions have extracted vast sums of money from the central government.

7

Conclusion

In this book, we have described the ideas and the results of the Russian mass privatization program. The two years since privatization began are not enough time to know how much it will boost the Russian economy. But enough time has elapsed to evaluate the main ideas, and to ask whether privatization has put the country on a better development path.

In the introduction, we outlined the three main ideas of Russian privatization: that people respond to incentives, that political influence is the fundamental economic problem of transition economies, and that the government owns nothing outright and hence the consent of all stakeholders is essential for successful reforms. How did these ideas fare in practice?

Privatization vividly demonstrated that incentives work. When given an opportunity to own shares in their companies, managers and workers grabbed it. They could have let privatization pass by, yet few did. When given a chance to claim their vouchers, virtually all Russians did so. They did not, as widely predicted, dismiss privatization as a government trick or view vouchers as worthless scrip. Millions have gone on to invest their vouchers in shares of companies and in mutual funds, so Russia now has more private shareholders than all of Western Europe put together. In fact, most of the two percent of the people who have not used their vouchers lived in the regions where local *governments* actively resisted privatization. The Russian people have evidently responded to opportunities when not stopped by their leaders.

Privatization is of course only one route by which market reforms unleashed new energy in the Russian economy. Millions of people, most of them under thirty-five, have quit their dead-end jobs in decrepit industries and joined the service economy. They are buying, transporting, and selling goods that consumers actually want to buy, whether these goods are produced at home or abroad. They are feverishly creating financial markets, by finding and buying up the shares that workers and impatient citizens are selling, and consolidating control of firms. This is hardly a group that does not respond to incentives.

The second idea tested by privatization was that depoliticization is a prerequisite for genuine economic change. Even before privatization started, price liberalization, which involved no more than the removal of bureaucrats and politicians from price setting, eliminated queues and shortages in a matter of weeks. In the few sectors where prices were not liberalized, such as energy, shortages persisted, and politicians issuing export quotas, together with criminals and company managers, made millions stealing oil and exporting it at market prices.

With privatization, there is a similar divergence of experiences depending on whether or not the government stayed involved. When the ministries moved away from telling them what to do, firms began to change their product lines, rationalize production, and more generally restructure. But when politicians retained control, as in the case of agriculture or urban real estate, the result has been corruption and continued economic stagnation. The devastating effects of political control continue to be felt in every part of the Russian economy.

The privatization process itself illustrated the importance of depoliticization. When the government played a minimal role in this process, privatization worked extremely well. Firms were sold at voucher auctions without major scandals, they often acquired large investors, and share consolidation through the private market started immediately afterwards. Individuals sold their vouchers when they pleased, invested them in voucher investment funds which blossomed under relatively light government regulations, and freely participated in voucher auctions. In contrast, when the government became heavily involved, it was to prevent large investors from buying shares, to rig investment tenders, to give credits to companies which they used to buy their own shares, or to put shares in ministerially controlled financial-industrial groups. We are not claiming here that a total absence of government regulation is required for things to work. Rather, starting from the extremely aggressive regulatory stance that Russian politicians typically take, less political influence usually leads to better outcomes.

The third idea was that the government did not really own Russian companies, and that privatization required first and foremost the co-optation of the stakeholders. This meant winning them over by rewarding each stakeholder's power to stop privatization with control and cash flow rights. Generous as the privatizers tried to be to the stakeholders, they typically still came up short of what was necessary to ensure political and economic support. Worker and manager benefits ended up being larger than originally planned, and even so the privatization program passed the Parliament by only a hair. During the implementation of the program, it became increasingly clear that the central government could at best offer guidelines, since managers and local governments had the power to block its efforts. Had the privatizers not understood this fact, there would have been no privatization in Russia; only continued theft of state assets. To a large extent, privatization gave cash flow rights to those who had significant control rights in the first place.

The three main ideas of the Russian privatization were thus soundly confirmed by experience. Mass privatization worked largely as designed, and was completed successfully in less than two years. Without reviewing all the details, we want to stress in this chapter three types of benefits of this program: economic, institutional, and political. These benefits, we believe, have put Russia on a more attractive development path than was even conceivable in 1991.

Privatization has radically altered the ownership structure of Russian firms, and moved it much closer to efficiency. Firms are now legally controlled not by politicians with perverse interests and no concerns for efficiency, but by managers and outside investors. Because they have cash flow rights as well, these new owners have a much greater interest in maximizing profits than the ministries ever had. Although the corporate governance system is far from perfect, it is developing rapidly. In response to market pressures, firms are separating from the government and beginning to restructure. Moreover, this is happening not just to a few showcase firms with foreign investors, but to tens of thousands of firms throughout the economy.

Russia is also poised to further reform its institutions. Privatization has created a substantial class of property owners who are increasingly demanding reforms that assure protection of property and contract enforcement. The most important of these reforms is the creation of commercial laws covering a whole range of market transactions. Even the Parliament is actively involved in the production of such laws. Similarly, rising crime, which was a predictable response to the government's failure to protect property, has moved from political obscurity in 1992 to the top of political concerns. Since most crime is targeted at property, property owners are leading the political push for tough measures to control crime. While Russia will not turn into a law-and-order paradise in the near future, the interests engendered by privatization are using their economic and political resources to press hard for institutional reforms.

But perhaps the most significant consequences of privatization are political. Privatization has created a class of property owners who have become the clear economic beneficiaries, and political supporters, of further liberalization of the Russian economy and society. This class is not limited to a few brokers and traders driving BMWs around Moscow, as some Western observers would like to believe. These property owners include the 40 million Russians holding shares in privatized firms and in mutual funds who want their investment protected. They also include the millions of people working for the growing service sector. In a country of 100 million voters, these are significant constituencies, which will throw their weight behind such critical reforms as land privatization, stabilization, and free trade. More importantly, the new property owners support the economic reformers who continue their struggle against communists and nationalists. Privatization and reform have created powerful political interests that are injecting some liberalism into Russian politics.

How significant are these accomplishments of privatization? Would Russia have been a better country with a different approach to reform? There was, after all, an alternative approach that was favored by many influential people. Property reform, as well as stabilization, should have been slow and deliberate, they said. Commercial institutions, including the legal system, should have been built before any firms were privatized. Privatization itself should have minimized giveaways to insiders and the public, and focused instead on finding good buyers one at a time. Even this method should have been applied carefully, with a few pilot projects before the actual roll-out. With slow and deliberate reform, Russia might have seen occasional but thorough restructuring, well-planned market institutions, and less volatile and divisive politics. But what would really have happened in Russia if this approach had been used?

The answer is simple: nothing good. Without price liberalization, there would still be very little food or consumer goods on store shelves. With slow reform there would have been no privatization either. The few major foreign companies that tried to buy Russian firms in 1991 typically failed to obtain all the necessary bureaucratic signatures and went home. Political control of the process was just too heavy-handed. Many of these same buyers actually came back and negotiated deals with the Russian firms after they were privatized. In 1991, the political support for such acquisitions did not exist, since insiders wanted to keep the firms for themselves. In fact, if Chubais had not pushed the privatization program through as fast as he did, the conservative opposition to any privatization effort would have organized itself much better, and continued state ownership would have been assured. The Russian economy would still be managed by politicians, the budget would be sinking from ever-growing subsidies, and managers would be sticking to business as usual. There would be no hope for industrial restructuring, or, for that matter, for the Russian economy.

The reform experience of both Russia and Eastern Europe reveals the pitfalls of the gradualist approach. In fact, Russia used the slow approach to land reform. Traditional agricultural ministries were put in charge of the process. Collective farms were to be restructured, and only privatized afterwards. In a pilot project, six collective farms in Nizhny Novgorod were broken up. In the meantime, the rest of Russian agriculture remained state-owned, consumed perhaps a fifth of the national income in subsidies, and continued its inexorable decline. Collective agriculture has failed in Russia. Today, people are eating thanks only to imports and to the millions of tiny private land plots on which they grow food.

This experience is representative of the rest of Eastern Europe. Countries that implemented fast reforms, such as the Czech Republic and Poland, have begun to grow. Countries such as Bulgaria, Belarus and Ukraine, which were the very slow reformers, are facing economic collapse. Ukraine's living standards have fallen significantly below Russia's, having been comparable in 1991. Even in China, the darling of the gradualist school, most state firms are nearly bankrupt and are nothing but a cancer on an otherwise growing economy. Without privatization, most of Russia would be like that cancer.

It is even more naive to suppose that Russia would have built free market institutions without privatization. In 1992, neither the public nor politicians had any interest in commercial laws, the stock market, corporate governance, or, for that matter, protection of private property. These issues became important not because Western academics said so, but because privatization created economic actors whose welfare turned critically on the resolution of these issues. In 1991, these actors were too few to influence economic policy; in 1994, following privatization, there were millions of them and they were getting richer. Privatization has created an economically and politically powerful lobby for institutional reform. Economic institutions cannot possibly precede the reallocation of property from the government, because people do not care about these institutions until, as property owners, they have an economic interest. With slow and deliberate reform, this interest would not have come about, and neither would the institutions.

Would Russian politics be less divisive and volatile with slower reforms? Go-slow advocates are surely right that price liberalization has hit the poorer members of society the hardest, and that their welfare payments have not kept up with inflation. Reforms would have been more popular, and politics less divisive, if social payments received a higher priority. Part of the problem, of course, was that the anti-reformers insisted on pumping resources into industry and agriculture, which left less for social programs. The reformers had no choice but to go along. Inflation would have been much faster if social spending had grown as well. Still, higher social spending would have paid off in greater political stability.

At the same time, it is easy to underestimate the political benefits of rapid reform. Reform has produced millions of beneficiaries who are the most important countervailing force to both left- and right-wing extremism. Such extremism would have existed in Russia anyway, because it is bred largely by the frustrated nationalism of a declining empire. Still, despite the prevalence of communists and nationalists, the current Parliament is more responsible and willing to work than the previous one. The new Russian politicians may not be as attractive as one would like, but the old ones, who would have continued their dominance under gradualist reforms, were worse. Without economic reform, there would be far fewer liberals to stand up to them.

Nor is the politics of countries with gradualist reform that attractive. The fast-reforming Czech Republic and Poland, despite some political setbacks, probably have among the most enlightened and least divisive politics in Eastern Europe. Ukraine, in contrast, kept its communist hacks through its years of nonreform. Hungary, its gradualist reforms notwithstanding, brought the old communists to power in an election. In China, the paragon of slow reforms, the communists never left. The sad truth is that any country shedding communism has to contend with political volatility.

Will the reform constituency eventually prevail in Russia? Will Russia emerge as the next tiger of economic development? Will it instead go through a long period of Latin American stagnation, as politicians tighten their control of the economy and the public pays for it through continued inflation and low living standards? Or will Russia revert to even a worse form of statism, of the sort advocated by its nationalists? The experience of Eastern Europe shows how important it is to get some reforms going, both because markets build on themselves, and because of the political interests they engender. Although pseudo-communist governments have come to power in Poland, Hungary, and Lithuania, the basic pro-market orientation of economic policy has not been reversed. Has Russia gone far enough down the road of economic reform that even a bad government cannot change the policy 180 degrees?

Our answer to the last question is Yes. Over the next decade, Russia is extremely likely to have governments more conservative than Gaidar's, and probably even more conservative than Chernomyrdin's. But price liberalization and privatization have shown that markets work in Russia, and that much good comes out of markets. People now own private property and want to own more. Russia has probably already reached the point where, at worst, it would get itself into the traditional Latin American scenario, in which politicians still do a lot of damage, but the living standards are higher than under socialism. With another year or two of reforms, as their economic benefits are felt more powerfully, and as the pro-market political constituency becomes stronger, Russia might be out of the woods. It would then be at the point of Latin America in the 1980s, where market ideas come to dominate, and where the economy is poised for economic growth. That may be an optimistic prediction, but it is not an unrealistic one. And even the possibility of this development path for Russia was unimaginable in 1991—before privatization.

Index

DATE DUE

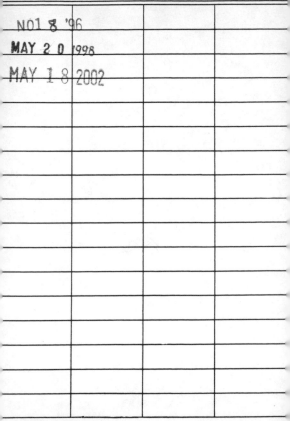

NO1 8 '96		
MAY 2 0 1998		
MAY 1 8 2002		